LIBRARY

Shepherd of the Hills
Lutheran Church
500 Blake Road

Presented By

Library Budget
1977

MY WAR
with
WORRY

MY WAR
with
WORRY

Tay Thomas

Published by
chosen books
Distributed by Word Books • Waco, Texas 76703

283
.TL

Scripture quotations identified KJV are from the King James Version
of the Bible. Scripture quotations identified TEV are from the
Today's English Version of the Bible. Copyright © American Bible
Society 1976.

Sketches by Lou Prickett, Anchorage, Alaska
Jacket photograph by Sam Kimura, Anchorage, Alaska

Library of Congress Cataloging in Publication Data

Thomas, Tay.
  My war with worry.

  1. Thomas, Tay. 2. Episcopalians—Biography.
3. Anchorage, Alaska—Earthquake, 1964-
Personal narratives. 4. Pentecostalism. I. Title.
BX5995.T4A33   283'.092'4 [B]   77-80669

ISBN 0-912376-19-8

*_2397_*

12-77 Lib Budget

To

My Mother and Father
who celebrated their 50th wedding anniversary
on September 18, 1976

and

Our daughter Anne and John Donaghy
married on September 18, 1976

Acknowledgments

My grateful thanks to Pat Michael for her countless hours of dedication to typing and retyping the manuscript; to the Reverend Chuck Eddy for his constant support and manuscript suggestions; to Catherine Marshall and Len LeSourd for their friendship and loving guidance; and my love and gratitude to a very special person—Elizabeth Sherrill. Without her sensitive understanding and special gift for editing, this book might never have been completed.

Tay Thomas

Contents

1. FLIGHT TO ADVENTURE   11
2. SCARED-Y CAT!   27
3. THE FEAR WITH NO NAME   42
4. WHY DON'T YOU FOLLOW ME?   52
5. A PILL TO SLEEP BY   61
6. THE SOLID GROUND   73
7. SPEAK THROUGH THE EARTHQUAKE   82
8. WIND THROUGH THE PINE TREES   100
9. WHITE-KNUCKLE FLIER   111
10. I GIVE YOU LOWELL AND HIS AIRPLANE   119
11. "LADIES AND GENTLEMEN . . ."   131
12. MY SECRET GARDEN   139

1.

Flight to Adventure

We rounded a narrow bend in the trail and another throat-catching vista of mountains opened before us, jagged white peaks standing sharp against a deep blue sky. Lowell, as always a few hundred feet ahead of me, turned and pointed to the view ahead. I managed a wan smile, struggling to rise from my almost overwhelming weariness. My husband was obviously elated, deeply happy to be penetrating an area he had dreamed of visiting for so long.

After four years of fighting government red tape, we had

succeeded in obtaining permission to visit one of the most remote and seldom visited countries on earth. Hunza was a semi-autonomous kingdom along the border between Pakistan and China, in the heart of the Himalayas. Its only links with the rest of the world were two narrow foot trails, one on either side of the Hunza River, covering the sixty-three miles from the nearest Pakistani village of Gilgit.

Lowell was walking vigorously, the distance between us widening steadily. His bulky brown jacket effectively concealed his lean, muscular build, but I could sense, watching his long strides and nimble dodging among the boulders, that the fifteen miles we had already walked that day were just a stroll for him.

They had felt like an eternity to me. Every muscle ached, and when I looked at the almost perpendicular trail in front of us, I wondered how I would find the strength to climb it. I should have been in top physical shape, partly because of the strenuous athletic life I shared with Lowell, but also because we had recently finished an arduous week-long trek with Afghan nomads, walking from five in the morning until three each afternoon across the barren desert of Afghanistan. I was proud that I had been strong enough to keep up with those toughened, perpetual wanderers. But now I was exhausted, and I couldn't understand it.

I felt like an inert bundle of clothing (and I must have looked it, in my shapeless quilted jacket and a pair of men's baggy brown corduroy pants), being pulled along like the baggage ponies by Lowell and our three Hunza guides. My feet, in their stiff leather boots, felt like two lead weights and every step became more of a struggle. I longed to climb onto one of the two shaggy ponies which had been fitted with saddles for riding, but I cringed at the memory of my one and only attempt.

I had pulled myself up into the saddle with gratitude, happy to get my tired feet off the ground. But it wasn't long before I discovered that these mountain beasts of burden walk on the very outer edge of the trail, a habit formed when they carry heavy loads which need the extra clearance space from the rock wall on the other side.

One hour of this tight-rope riding was all I could take; when the pony stumbled, dislodging stones which careened down the sheer mountain face to the river far below, I scrambled hastily off his back. I was shaking with fright, and Lowell turned back to reassure me. "You're better off walking," he said, and began to recall aloud stories he'd heard about pack animals falling from this trail to inevitable death a thousand feet below. As my knees turned to water, he added that a Pakistani official had warned him we would find the river bed strewn with the carcasses of dead horses and mules. Now he tells me, I thought, as I vowed to trust nothing but my own two legs from then on.

"It's these miserable rocks in the path," I muttered as I stumbled for the thousandth time. I simply had to keep my eyes off the view that so entranced Lowell, and on the ground in front of me. The ledge we were following grew even narrower. Every once in a while I inadvertently glanced to the left, and immediately regretted it—the edge of the cliff was inches from my foot, then a sheer drop to the roaring river.

I had always dreaded heights. I remembered the time I had followed Lowell up the steps of a fire tower in the Rocky Mountains. At the first landing I was so dizzy I'd collapsed in a trembling heap. An exasperated Lowell had to help me back down. He had never understood that feeling, and since one of his favorite sports was alpine skiing, on the steepest slopes possible, I had tried to overcome my fear of high places by learning to ski when we were first married, four years before, then tackling the roughest terrain right behind him. Doubtless my eagerness as a bride, anxious to please her husband in every way possible, had given me the determination to do it, but it had not healed my acrophobia.

I looked up ahead at Lowell, and decided to be as determined now—I so wanted to be a part of his new expedition. We had both been excited when starting from Gilgit the day before, feeling like a couple of kids setting out on a big adventure. We had had only an 11-mile walk that day because a battered World War II U.S. Army jeep was able to ferry us most of the thirty miles to our first overnight stop. We had been advised to take this trail on the eastern side of the river, passing through the mountain kingdom of Nagar, in order to take advantage of the lift in the jeep. The two sister states of Nagar and Hunza lay on either side of the wild torrent, rivals for centuries, but now united through the marriage of their ruling families. We would stay on the Nagar side until we reached the end of the trail, then cross the river to our destination in Hunza.

We had spent that first night in a deserted stone hut beside the trail, spreading our sleeping bags on the dirt floor. I had been delighted to see a fireplace, but appalled by the three slender twigs which were the entire fuel supply. These bare rock-strewn slopes were high desert country, with carefully cultivated apricot trees the only vegetation of any size.

It was December, definitely the wrong season of the year to head into the Himalayas, but nothing would stop Lowell when our travel permits came through from the Pakistani government. (Pakistan controlled Hunza's and Nagar's foreign affairs, and since this was a sensitive border area, few Westerners were allowed in.) The room was so cold, despite our miniature fire, that our breath hung in clouds above us, and the whitewashed adobe walls felt like sheets of ice. When one of our smiling, leather-faced guides brought us a pottery pitcher of hot water, along with a basin the size of a soup bowl, we both laughed. "Your bath is ready, Madam," Lowell mimicked a formal butler, and I replied, "Oh, after you, sir!" We ended up washing faces and hands only—if all our lodgings were to be this frigid, we would be returning to Gilgit in pretty dirty shape.

For supper that first night, we had bowls of canned beef stew (Lowell had purchased a small supply of English

"tins" in Gilgit to supplement local rations), the crisp flat
bread called chippattis and chipped white mugs of hot tea.
Fortunately for Lowell, I didn't feel hungry, so he ate most
of my portion as well. Our breakfast, after a shivering night
on the hard floor, consisted of the same bowls filled with a
glue-like porridge, along with mugs of instant coffee. Lunch,
eaten as we walked, was a handful of local apricots and a
chocolate bar apiece.

On and on we plodded, up another steep incline, down a
treacherous slope of loose scree, the ponies and I struggling
to keep our balance. Around another corner, and up again,
the trail ahead a thin twisting line across the steep rocky
slope. When would we ever get to that day's stopping place?
Our guides were reassuring and colorful companions with
their surefooted strides and red-dyed mustaches. But since
they spoke no English, it was useless to ask "how much
further?" We found out later that we had done a "double
march" that day, almost twenty-two miles: learning that the
hut which we were supposed to have slept in would be in
use, the guides had simply pushed on to the next stop, the
town of Nagar. Nagar was just across the river from Baltit,
our final destination, and the capital of Hunza.

Double marches—that seemed to be the theme of our trip
so far, I reminisced, as I tried to keep my mind off the
fatigue that was overwhelming me. I thought about the
many unforeseen miles we had covered in our single-engine
plane before reaching Pakistan. With different fuel require-
ments from those of commercial airliners, we often found
ourselves forced to fly on to another airfield in search of the
80-octane gas we needed.

When we originally planned this year-long flight from
Europe down through Africa and across the Middle East to
India and then Australia, we were both determined to keep
our schedule flexible. We did not want to be tied to traditional tourist routes and hectic timetables; we were looking
for interesting, off-the-beaten-track places and people, and
we'd found plenty of both. Although there were days when

it seemed we flew on (or walked!) endlessly, there had also been peaceful interludes in idyllic settings such as Marrakesh, Jerusalem, Cyprus, Istanbul, Teheran . . .

The frightening rattle of cascading rocks and the shouts of our guides brought me back to the present with a shock. My heart seemed to stop as I jerked my head up, scanning the steep scree above me. I would have to decide within seconds which way to run in order to get away from one of the frequent avalanches of stone set off by mountain goats.

Frantically I scanned the cloud of dust above us to determine which way the stones and boulders were headed. I knew I must move immediately, but as panic welled inside me, legs and brain seemed paralyzed. At that moment several large rocks struck the trail just behind me, and I scampered forward with a burst of energy I had thought was long expended. Seconds later we all stood together, frightened and quiet, watching the trail behind us vanish beneath a giant waterfall of mountainside debris. And what if the trail ahead, I thought anxiously, were to be wiped out in the same way?

That instant of desperate scrambling was followed by hours more of walking, climbing, stumbling, and then a new concern—descending darkness. Each moment it was becoming increasingly difficult to see the path. I was about to sit down and refuse to take another step when a full moon suddenly popped out from behind a distant peak. How strange that such a simple thing as moonlight could rejuvenate one's spirits so! A half hour later we rounded a bend and found ourselves in the small, dark village of Nagar —a handful of lightless stone huts, surrounded by terraced fields and dominated by a large building sitting on a hill beyond the town.

A few mangy, vociferous dogs were the only signs of life as we straggled down that dirt "main street," but I started up the final hill with high hopes. The building ahead of us, Lowell assured me, was the palace of the Mir of Nagar, where we'd been invited to spend the night. Excitement dulled fatigue, and we were astounded to discover polo fields all around us. We learned later that this sport originated here, and had been introduced to the Western world by Marco Polo on his return from China along this ancient trade route.

At the ornately carved wooden door of the palace, we were greeted by a servant in a long wool robe, who led us directly to a rather bleak guest room. Two beds and two bureaus lined the usual whitewashed walls, and a very small fireplace was obviously to be our only source of heat. There were no curtains, no rug, no other furniture. "Oh dear," I turned to Lowell, "I expected much fancier things in the palace of a Mir."

"Listen, you're lucky you have a bed tonight," Lowell replied. 'We never saw beds in Tibet." And from his experience as the veteran explorer he admonished me, the typical American suburbanite, to remember that every stick of furniture in that "palace" had to be brought in along that same trail we'd just covered, on the backs of ponies or mules.

Thoroughly chastened, I was sinking onto one of the beds, when a knock on the door brought me back to my weary, blistered feet. Another man, dressed in the same simply styled warm-looking robe, welcomed us politely in good English. He was the major-domo of the palace, he said, and he was welcoming us on behalf of the Mir, who was unfortunately detained on a visit to another part of his tiny kingdom. He added that we were expected in the dining room, for dinner with the Mir's son, immediately.

As much as I longed to collapse on that bed, there had been an imperious sound to that word *immediately*. So we washed ourselves as best we could in the small pan of warm water he left with us, then hurried down a narrow, icy-cold dark corridor to an equally cold dark dining room. Flickering candles on the table and in metal sconces along the walls revealed a long, nearly bare dining table and, sitting among many empty chairs, one very small boy.

He was huddled in the usual wool robe and also wore a cap of the same material. It was something like a beret, but with a rolled rim, the distinguishing headgear, we were to discover, of all the men in both the Hunza and Nagar principalities. I might have thought it rude for a child to sit at the dinner table with his hat on, but considering the bone-chilling temperature and the fact that his teeth were audibly chattering, I could only sympathize with the poor thing. Our sole communication with our young host throughout the meal was an occasional fleeting smile, for he apparently spoke no English and was obviously suffering besides from agonizing shyness.

Despite the fact that I had eaten only a few apricots and a chocolate bar since breakfast, I simply did not feel hungry. Just too tired, I decided. Still . . . there was something strange about this sudden lack of appetite. It was too dark to see what was on the plate that a servant placed before me, but as I lifted the first forkful to my lips, a wave of nausea swept over me. How silly, when I'd cheerfully eaten more foreign fare with the Pygmies in their jungle home. I'd never been a picky eater, and seldom had an upset stomach, even when traveling.

"It's chicken," Lowell said sensing my hesitation. "Pretty stringy," he added, "but these chickens run around the yard until the moment they're grabbed for the pot." That did it! I wanted nothing more to do with food, just that waiting bed to fall into.

The next day's journey from Nagar to Baltit, capital village of Hunza, was a brief one, but the most challenging of the entire trek. We had to cross the three-hundred-yard-wide river between the two kingdoms and the only way was via a bridge that had apparently been constructed for Marco Polo and gone unrepaired ever since. Two ancient ropes swung between the rock walls, about fifty feet above the raging water, sagging in the center dangerously close to the white froth. Thinner, badly frayed-looking lines formed cross-ties at three or four-foot intervals and supported a series of wooden slats. The rotting ropes were bad enough, but the number of missing or broken boards, leaving gaping holes to step across, had me backing away in terror.

"Great pictorial climax to our hike here!" Lowell shouted to me as, cameras hanging ready around his neck, he started across.

Now I was angry as well as scared. "You're always thinking of the stupid pictures!" I shouted back, but he was already halfway over, hanging onto the ropes, bouncing across the holes between the slats. "Please wait for me," I added weakly, as the bridge swayed wildly back and forth beneath his weight.

It was true that we were depending on good pictures to pay for our trip. We had received partial financing from NBC television and the *National Geographic* magazine to get our dream Flight to Adventure off the ground, and we would have to go home with the best photographic record possible. But there were times when it seemed to me that our "third companion"—the film equipment—got all the consideration.

Lowell had reached the far side and was getting his cameras ready for action. "I can't do it," I wailed, "you've got to help me!" Obviously he couldn't hear me over the roar of that angry river because he simply waved for me to start on over. I took a deep breath, grabbed the ropes, and cautiously eased my weight onto the first slat. Maybe if I moved slowly and gently, the bridge wouldn't swing so badly.

Another step, and then my heart seemed to come into my throat. Those slender ropes to which I was clinging for life itself, were thickly coated with ice. The slats too, as I tentatively eased the other foot forward, were slick with frozen spray from the river.

Clutching the slippery ropes, placing my feet with infinite caution, I inched forward. But no matter how slowly I moved, the swaying of that demonic bridge increased, feeding on itself like rippling waves. Now the planks were jumping up and down beneath my feet, faster and faster, while the whole contraption swung dizzily from side to side. In the center, where the bridge sagged sharply toward the churning water less than thirty feet below, the ice was thicker than ever. And suddenly I was faced with a wide gap between the slats—one piece was missing entirely—the next dangled splintered and useless.

I stopped, gloves freezing to their icy handhold, feet dancing on those chattering slats. For the first time I was really seeing that raging torrent of water, so close that I could feel drops of freezing spray. Until then I had made a tremendous effort to keep my eyes glued to the wooden planking, but now there was nothing beyond my feet except white foam, boiling caldrons of gray whirlpools, roaring waterfalls of water, and ice-coated rocks.

I panicked completely, clinging to the ropes, yelling, "Help me!" Lowell had been taking movies of my progress and only stopped long enough to call back encouragingly, "Come on, honey, you can make it!"

I was sobbing now. "I can't!" I cried, very close to hysterics. And apparently they believed me at last, for one of our guides came back across the bridge toward me, fast and sure-footed. He put his strong arms about me and half dragged, half carried me across.

With my feet safely on Hunza soil, I felt a wild mixture of emotions. Relief, shame over my poor performance as an "explorer," irritation at Lowell. He seemed quite unaware that my life had just been saved, and kept raving on about the fantastic pictures he'd gotten. I was only somewhat mollified when he added, "Dear, you've just covered the worst trail I've ever seen in my life, worse than anything I came across in Tibet."

The home of the Mir of Hunza was similar to that of his brother-in-law in Nagar, but better furnished and more modern. When I spotted a piano in the living room, I could only think of Lowell's comment and feel sorry for the animals who had had to carry that load! Despite such western touches though, there was still no plumbing, heat or electricity. The home was cold and empty—no Mir in residence there, either. For obvious reasons he had gone south to Karachi for the winter.

Our guest room was almost identical to the one we had just left, miserably cold and with the usual five or six slim twigs for our daily fuel ration. This time, however, the dining room too was warmed by a small fire. I hoped my appetite might improve as much as the temperature, and Lowell was delighted when the major-domo announced they had slaughtered a yak just for us. "Yak tastes like buffalo," Lowell said. "Only, remember he was also running about this morning, so expect to chew a lot." To my dismay, that same nauseous feeling had crept up again at the very mention of food. I have to eat something, I thought, and maybe it won't be all that bad. It was—like oily shoe leather. I settled for a little rice and tea.

We went to bed right after supper but, tired as I was and muscles still aching from the long hike of the day before, I could not fall asleep. Lowell had a maddening way of dropping off instantly, regardless of where he was, or what had happened during the day. So I lay quietly, trying to ignore his gentle snores, thinking back on all of our recent experiences, wondering when I would ever again enjoy a warm bath.

I wondered too about the almost constant exhaustion that had fallen like a heavy blanket over me. I'd been tired before, even worn out, but I'd never experienced such a constant sense of weariness. I tried to remember when I was first aware of it—maybe after we landed at Gilgit? That night we had eaten dinner with the local mayor. It had been the usual meal of stringy, tough chicken with rice, and I had not been able to swallow a bite. In fact—that's when I had first felt the nausea, but had dismissed it as a queasy stomach after a rough flight. Now, lying in this icebox of a room in Hunza, I knew this was not the reason. I was never airsick.

Then what in the world was the matter with me? I hadn't been ill. Not even a cold. My body was functioning perfectly normally, except for—despite the freezing air in the room I sat bolt upright on the bed. Pregnant. I was pregnant! I was sure of it, thinking back now on the subtle signs that suddenly fit into place.

I had never even considered such a thing: for the first three years of our marriage Lowell and I had tried to have a child, without success. We'd consulted several doctors, who could suggest nothing. There was nothing physically wrong, they told us—with some couples it often takes a longer time. And so a year ago we'd decided to concentrate on a life of travel instead.

I wriggled out of my sleeping bag to shake Lowell awake. "What's up?" he mumbled.

"Guess what!" I was bursting with my wonderful news. "You just won't believe it, but I'm pregnant!"

Lowell groaned and burrowed deeper into his down-filled sack. "Good grief, why did you have to pick now?" He yawned, sighed deeply, and the next instant was asleep again. Why did *I* have to pick now? Darn him, I thought, as I went back to bed. He had something to do with it, too!

And then the full realization swept over me. I was two—three—months pregnant, in the heart of one of the most primitive, harsh, and isolated areas on this planet. Our only link with the nearest semblance of civilization was that treacherous sixty-three-mile trail, which by Lowell's own admission was the worst he'd ever seen. Why did I have to be here, of all places—now that the one thing I had hoped for most in all those four years had happened.

I simply could not go back by that horrendous route. Even if I could get back across that bridge, which I knew I couldn't, there was that narrow path: that sickening drop to the river, the constantly falling rock. No, I would never be able to face it again, knowing our baby's life was in the balance too. There must be some other way out, and I lay awake for hours clutching at any idea that came to mind. They'd carve an airstrip out of the sheer mountain slopes and Lowell would fly our plane in! A Pakistani helicopter might be able to come to the rescue. I needed to be rescued, badly, and Lowell would arrange something. On that comforting conclusion I finally fell asleep.

Things so often look brighter at the start of a new day. Lowell, wide awake, was as delighted as I with my news of the night before. We shared our excitement over our meager breakfast, but when I broached the subject of alternatives to hiking out, he shook his head.

"You've got to be sensible, honey. There's no way they could make a place to land a plane here." And he simply laughed at the helicopter idea. "You've forgotten that we're over 7,000 feet now, and the passes we came over are much higher. No 'copter could possibly handle those heights." There went my thin shred of hope, and breaking into tears, I told him I could never face that terrible trail again, knowing I was pregnant. He was obviously unsure as to how to handle my present emotional state. At last he suggested I spend the day in bed while he visited Baltit alone. He had made plans the evening before for a full day of sightseeing and picture-taking.

I lay in my sleeping bag for what seemed endless hours. A pathetic little heap of ashes was soon all that remained of the fire. I remembered the roaring blazes we used to have in my family's oversized fireplace. I was bothered too by my dirty sweater and pants. The cold was so intense that we had not undressed since we left Gilgit. At home, Mother had been strict about cleanliness—at the slightest sign of soil, clothing had been whisked away by the laundress, to be returned ironed and spotless overnight. And I could almost feel the soothing hot water in the bathtub next to my old room.

I ached with loneliness, and my stomach felt nauseous again. I thought about when we were sick as kids—we'd be tucked at once between clean white sheets. I burst into tears and sobbed, my face buried in the grubby cloth of my sleeping bag. My father had been so proud over my taking this trip with Lowell. "I always knew you were a brave girl who loved adventure," he had said, beaming. From the time we were small children Dad had trained me and my brothers and sister to be fearless and independent. Bedtime usually meant an adventure story, either read aloud from a book or told from his own experience, and all the games he played with us were designed to develop courage and resourcefulness.

I sobbed even more at this memory of the past. I'm not brave, Dad, I'm a total coward. I've always been afraid, my whole life. You told us to act as if fear didn't exist, and it would go away. But it didn't, Dad, not for me. I tried to pretend, but I felt so scared inside. And I'm tired of acting courageous when I don't feel that way. I don't even know why I'm here, except that I love Lowell so much I'd follow him to the moon. And I'm especially scared of that trail.

All the fears that I'd succeeded in holding in check on the way in rose now to the surface. In the midst of my wracking sobs, my churning stomach reminded me of my even greater concern. I wanted a baby so very badly. How could I possibly repeat that trip without losing the most precious gift I would ever be given?

There was a knock on the door, and I had to stop crying long enough to accept a bowl of thin, tepid broth and some lukewarm tea from a concerned and puzzled major-domo. It was lunchtime, he said, didn't I want something more to eat? Only lunchtime! Surely it must be late afternoon by now—just a little weak winter sunshine filtered through the two slit-like windows. Yes, I'd love more to eat, I thought. Some of Mother's thick home-made soup and crisp garden salad, served on her lovely china. And maybe a tall glass of cold milk. I couldn't remember when we'd last had fresh vegetables, and we hadn't tasted fresh milk since we left the United States nearly eleven months before. Had it really been that long? I felt close to tears again, so I hastily thanked the uncomfortable man and tried to eat what he'd brought.

I must have fallen asleep then, because I awoke to hear Lowell come in. The room was pitch black, but I could feel that I had swollen eyes and a tear-streaked face. Lowell lit the candles, revitalized the fire, then brought me a towel and the usual bowl of water.

As I tried to repair my messy face, Lowell's gentle and loving self broke through the veneer of the hardy explorer. "I've been thinking about our trip out all day," he told me, "and I've found the perfect solution." I could almost hear the roar of an airplane engine as I sat up to hear every word. "I had a long talk with the local mayor," he went on, "and he says we should go out on the Hunza trail, on this side of the river." My heart sank and I fell back onto the bed again. "Honestly, dear," Lowell pleaded. "He says it's a much safer and easier route, mostly through villages, with only a few narrow stretches to get over. The mayor will lend you his best riding horse for the whole journey, and we'll plan it in short, easy stages."

I was catching Lowell's optimism when, from somewhere in the recesses of my mind I remembered someone saying, "Pregnant women shouldn't ride horseback."

I started to cry again. Lowell tried a new tack: "Why don't I have some food brought right here to us, and some of their delicious apricot wine?" I tearfully acquiesced, although the thought of more yak meat was enough to make me grab for the pot under the bed.

I let Lowell eat the yak that night, while I nibbled on rice and chippattis. I also drank three glasses of their home-brewed wine, not knowing it was lethal, especially at that altitude. By the time Lowell returned to our plans for leaving, I was in an alcoholic euphoria. "We'll spend three or four more days here while you rest up," he said, "and I can get lots of great picture material." He described the arrangements he could make to be sure the bungalows used by travelers along the route would be free for us. "Sounds like fun," I said nonchalantly, and dropped into a dreamless sleep.

We left the village of Hunza three days later, on a cold, clear morning. The sky was a deep blue, white plumes trailing from the peaks of the snow-covered mountains. Lowell was walking, using his cameras often as he exclaimed over the magnificent scenery and the groups of friendly Hunzacuts who lined the trail to see us off. I was riding a gentle, obviously well-trained horse, but I could not appreciate him or the beauty around us, so anxious was I over what the jogging of the ride might bring on.

It was a short ride that day, only ten miles to our first stop. It seemed a long way to me, though, as tension raced through my body with every jolt. That persistent phrase, "Pregnant women shouldn't ride horseback," repeated itself over and over in rhythm with the horse's hoof beats. We'd gone about five miles when the stomach cramps began. From then on every step of the trail was agony, mental as much as physical. When we finally dismounted in front of the usual one-room adobe building I could hardly wait to take my sleeping bag from the back of the baggage pony and crawl into it. But the cramps only increased in severity and I was convinced I was going to have a miscarriage right there in that hut in Hunza.

The early December darkness came, but sleep would not. Finally, close to exhaustion, my mind wandered to the little poem I'd pasted on the dashboard of our plane just before our first take-off from Paris:

> Peace be in thy home
> And in thy heart.
> Or if thou roam
> Earth's highways wide,
> The Lord be at thy side
> To bless and guide.

I had often glanced at that little verse while we were flying, feeling a vague sense of comfort from the words. Was there really a God? I wondered. And if so, did He know about Lowell and me and our unborn child, here in this wayside hut?

And if He knew . . . did He care?

2.

Scared-y Cat!

It was hot inside the little chapel, the Florida sun beating on the stained-glass windows. If I get through this without fainting, I thought, it will be a minor miracle. Lowell and I had arrived home from our fourteen-month Flight to Adventure just three days earlier, and I was still tired from the travel and time change. What perfect timing though— winding up all the details in Paris concerned with shipping our airplane home, flying on to New York, and then to Florida just in time for my sister's wedding. There had been little chance to visit with family and friends yet. But then it would take months to fill them in on even half of our experiences.

The organist began to play the traditional strains of the wedding processional, and I clutched my flowers, steadying myself for the walk down the aisle. My sister Frannie had been sweet to include me in the wedding party, although I had warned her that my six-months-pregnant condition would do little to enhance her lovely attendant gown. She assured me that it had a full skirt and I needn't worry. I'd also begged my mother (all this by transatlantic phone call from Paris) to order me a gigantic floral bouquet—something enormous that I could hide behind.

Crafty Mother! I thought, as I looked down at the wisp of tiny white roses between two slim strands of ivy. I suspected that she had selected this miniature arrangement on purpose. She and Dad had been deliriously happy over our news; they'd been as disappointed as we when the years passed with no sign of a grandchild, particularly since I was their eldest, and the first married. Now she was all too eager for the family and friends in the chapel to be aware of my expectant condition!

And why shouldn't the whole world know? Here we were, home safe and sound from our great adventure, and about to be parents as well! The obstetrician with whom we had checked in Karachi, an English nun, had assured us that the cramps I'd experienced in Hunza meant nothing serious: they'd been brought on more by worry, she suspected, than by horseback riding. Both Lowell and I wanted our baby born at home, so we had canceled our original lengthy flight plan to Australia and returned to Paris, flying in easy stages, but taking another route back so as to add to our pictorial story.

A nudge on my arm brought me back to the church ceremony. I'd been about to follow the bridesmaids to the side of the chancel, rather than stand beside the bride, as matron of honor. As the minister's voice chanted the familiar words of the marriage ceremony, my mind wandered again, back to those final three months of our aerial odyssey. We'd visited Arab sheikdoms along the Persian Gulf, and then made history of sorts by being the first small private plane to cross the vast Saudi Arabian desert. I had performed my usual navigational duties, plotting our course with the sole aid of irregular formations of sand dunes marked on our map for us by a pilot for an American oil company—the only identifiable land marks in that great mass of sand. And all the while fighting a wild craving for dill pickles!

From the coast of Oman, we flew on across the Red Sea to Cairo, where we encountered our first American tourists since leaving Karachi. We had flown for seven hours that day in hot, rough air over the Egyptian desert, refueling at a primitive wilderness airstrip with no chance for lunch. Going up in a crowded elevator that evening in a luxurious Cairo hotel, I had fainted. Several Americans helped Lowell get me to our room. One lady asked if I was sick and I'll never forget her face when Lowell said, "Oh no, she's just pregnant and we've been over the desert all day with no food." Here's a real pioneer type, the lady's face said: a daring soul who doesn't know the meaning of fear!

Frannie turned and laid her bridal bouquet in my arms. We were now at the most meaningful part of the ceremony, when she and Bob Haws would exchange their wedding vows. It was hard to believe that this lovely young woman in the flowing white organdy dress was my mischievous little tomboy of a sister. In fact, I couldn't remember ever seeing her in anything but blue jeans. Seven years younger than I, her world was strictly the out-of-doors, especially on horseback, though there was no sport in which she did not excel. Bob, standing by her side, was tall and handsome in his white Naval Airman's uniform. They had dated each other since the seventh grade.

I looked beyond Bob to his best man, my brother Tap. Six feet three, blond and strikingly handsome in his Marine dress whites, Tap was the middle one of us five children, four years younger than I. He most closely resembled our dad in character and temperament, and, more than any of the rest of us, epitomized the confidence, courage and individuality that Dad had always emphasized we must develop. He had barely squeaked through college—majoring in canoeing, the family used to say. He then enlisted in the Marine Corps and, after achieving highest honors as a marksman with his rifle, took on the challenge of learning to fly helicopters.

Standing behind Tap, looking decidedly uncomfortable in their role as ushers, were my two other brothers. Sam, just a year younger than I, also wore the Marine dress uniform. But Sam had a different kind of strength and courage from Tap's. He had the quiet confidence and endearing charm which made him a born leader of people. Larry, the attractive, shaggy-haired baby of the family, was a typical seventeen-year-old, easygoing and happy-go-lucky. Because he had been born so much later, he seemed free of the pressures laid on the rest of us, content to be a "regular guy." As the youngest, he'd gotten lots of loving, and during those later years when Larry was growing up, Dad was away from home much of the time, working long, demanding hours in his new position as Executive Vice President of Pan American Airways. All Dad's great energy, so much of which had once been directed to the training and molding of his children, had by then been channeled elsewhere.

"Training and molding"—perhaps the right words, but they do not in any way adequately describe the kind of life we led. We were close as a family: few parents in the 1930's spent as much time with their children as did ours. But then everything they did with their lives was different. We lived in the country club-oriented suburb of Greenwich, Connecticut, but Mother and Dad shunned association with this segment of the community. At a time when most young married women devoted their leisure to bridge and dinner parties, Mother was vice-chairman of the Republican Town Committee. She was also instrumental in starting a recreation center for the local black community when working with minorities was not a popular cause.

Dad was active in both state and national politics, serving as Republican National Committeeman from Connecticut for many years, and was eastern campaign manager for Wendell Willkie in the 1940 presidential election. He somehow found the time, too, to be one of the organizers of the Greenwich Boys Club, promoting sports activities for the youngsters in town who had no access to country club facilities. His own favorite sport was boxing—when Dad was lightweight champion at his college, he met Gene Tunney and they became lifelong friends. The first Tunney-Dempsey match was held outdoors in pouring rain five days after Mother and Dad were married, and Mom had to agree to a honeymoon interruption to sit in the downpour wearing her trousseau best. When I was born the following year, "Uncle Gene," then world heavyweight champion, became my godfather.

Dad was a nonconformist who left no doubt in his five children's minds that to be adventurous and self-reliant was the only approach to life. When we were small, story hour with him was our favorite time of day. He would read aloud to us from books on exploration—a dramatic account of a 1906 expedition to Tibet, a blood-curdling story of the man-eating lions of Tsavo, our favorite *Swiss Family Robinson* episodes. Dad's personal reminiscences, however, were even more fascinating—tales of his early adventures as a seventeen-year-old seaman shoveling coal below the decks of a naval barge in the North Sea during World War I, of his later travels through Africa and then all around the world. Although Dad could have had everything in life handed to him on a silver platter, he always chose to make his own way, often taking the hardest route possible.

As we grew older, we began to act out Dad's African adventures, starting with a sleeping tent in the back yard. He supplied appropriate background sounds, prowling through nearby bushes late at night imitating the growl of a lion, or shooting off a gun so that pellets rained down around us. Later we took turns using Dad's guns, with an elaborate shooting gallery of perched bottles and hanging cans.

When wartime gas rationing was imposed, Dad conceived the idea of supplying the family with light, one-cylinder motorcycles. We must have been quite a sight on our frequent family outings—Dad slowly leading the procession on his huge heavy red monster, complete with sidecar for little Larry, followed closely by Mother with Frannie riding behind her, then we three older children on our miniature models.

Most family games had a moral to them, and the moral was always the same: fear exists only in the imagination. Many nights, after listening together to a scary radio program like "Inner Sanctum," Dad would challenge us: "I'll give any of you a quarter if you'll go down to the basement alone right now, and walk through it without turning on the lights." This was a formidable proposition because our basement was not only as dark and creaky as most basements, but it was there that Dad kept his African trophies. Huge hairy stuffed heads lined the walls, glassy eyes staring blindly. There was a wild buffalo with curling horns, and an enormous alligator whose jaws seemed spread in a leering smile. The rhino in particular, with his hideous snout and tiny bloodshot eyes, haunted my nightmares. As we grew older, Sam and Tap and even Frannie grew rich on this game. But much as I longed to make Dad proud of me, and often as I told myself these were only lifeless skins and bits of glass, I could never force myself down there in the dark.

Dad's favorite game was one we played at our winter retreat in Florida. A thick stretch of tropical growth protected our small house from the ocean's spray. Dad spent long hours hacking out a passage with a machete, then proudly dubbed it the "Jungle Path." Now came the true test of courage— after dark we were told to take a small shovel and pail, negotiate the path all the way to the beach, fill the pail with sand and bring it back to Dad. The reward for this feat was upped to fifty cents. Part of the game, of course, was Dad's constant imitation of animal sounds and ominous rustling of bushes all along the way. Frannie and Larry, young as they were, made brave attempts, and were praised for their brief sorties. Sam and Tap always triumphantly returned with the sand, but I remained indoors, feeling like the coward I was.

Of course I knew there were no lions or tigers in our "jungle," but I was painfully aware of the very real wildlife I occasionally saw on my way to the beach in the daytime— snakes slithering across the path (once I nearly stepped on a deadly coral snake); armadillos and skunks scampering away; large, hairy spiders dangling face-high from the branches.

Another popular pastime during our visits to Florida was an "expedition" into the Everglades. At that time, before urban development had reached the state, a wilderness of scrub pines, palmettoes, and mangrove swamps lay just across the river from our island home. The area was inhabited by alligators, snakes, wild pigs, and other creatures guaranteed to lend authenticity to any safari.

"Time to get under way," Dad would call out, and we'd all come running, often with friends in tow, clutching an assortment of pith helmets, machetes, and guns. Dad borrowed a battered old truck from a neighbor, and we piled in or perched on fenders and occasionally the roof, depending on the size of the crowd. As we sputtered off down the driveway, Mother stayed behind to fill a vital role in this enterprise—calling the local sheriff to come look for us if we weren't home by dark. And most of the time the poor, much-abused truck did break down, as if on cue from Dad, forcing us to walk four or five miles toward home before the sheriff could come to the rescue.

On one of these outings Dad found himself face to face with an adventure he had not programmed. The radiator of the ancient truck had overheated, a normal occurrence, and Dad took the usual container to a nearby stream for water. A large board lay across the deepest water hole, and holding the can in one hand, Dad lifted the wooden obstruction with the other. The next second he was staring into the beady eyes of a deadly cottonmouth water moccasin. He froze, not even daring to call for help, knowing that the slightest movement or sound on his part would cause the snake to strike. He could only desperately hope that one of us would see the situation and think to get out the shotgun. One well-aimed blast from that heavy gun would knock the snake's head right off. Dad's training of us all in marksmanship probably saved his life that day: Tap saw the reptile, grabbed his own small BB gun, took careful aim, and killed the snake by hitting it squarely in the eye. If the little pellet had been off by even a quarter-inch, a very live but infuriated snake would undoubtedly have lashed out and bitten Dad.

When he was not with his children, Dad's favorite activity was flying. At that time he worked for a railroad company, but he spent many of his free hours flying as a passenger in the tiny, single-engine, cloth-covered planes of those days. Sometimes the pilot was Roscoe Turner, Al Williams or Eddie Rickenbacker, all aviator friends he admired greatly.

Whenever our family went to Florida, the entire household except for Dad traveled by train, including the cook, a nursemaid, us five children and assorted animals. (Once one of our cats gave birth to kittens in an upper bunk, and on another occasion Sam and Tap emptied a dining car of its occupants in seconds when they released a small alligator in the aisle.) Only when we were finally well-settled, would Dad fly in to join us. We children always watched wide-eyed as his small plane landed in the nearest open clearing. I was grown up before I realized that Mother was the real hero of those travels!

Dad eventually decided that he had to learn to fly himself. He found a seaplane based on Long Island Sound near our home, with an instructor willing to take him on. It wasn't long before he soloed, and then all home activities ceased whenever he buzzed over our house. We kids also hung around the hangar, hoping for an occasional ride, but happy just to help pull the plane to the float. Of course the time soon came when the two older boys wanted to take lessons and solo, too. To my great joy, I was often allowed to go along in the back seat just for the ride. My lack of self-confidence was such that it never occurred to me to ask if I could take piloting lessons too.

The little seaplane was by no means our only contact with flying—we took frequent flights in other small planes, and after Dad went to work with Pan American, long trips in bigger ones as well.

When we were home there was a constant stream of household guests. Sundays, in particular, were considered "open house" days, and Mother never knew how many would appear, or what the mix would be. Guests could range all the way from the prime minister of Pakistan or presidential candidate Wendell Willkie to gun-inventor and ex-convict "Carbine Williams."

While our life probably looked carefree and exciting to these visitors, it was actually one of considerable regimentation and strict discipline, of frequent periods when we children were left home alone with an unsmiling governess and an irritable elderly cook. This was common practice at that time, and it was also a time when babies were picked up only to be fed, and then on a rigid four-hour schedule. It was a time when one was not demonstrative with affection, when children were taught not to cry or show negative feelings, no matter how justified.

As toddlers, Sam and I must have spent most of our day in the care of a German nanny because I still remember what happened one evening when we were taken to Mother and Dad just before bedtime. As we said our good nights, they looked at each other in great concern; then in an unusual break from routine, the nanny was excused and we were asked "How do you say this?" or "What's the word for that?" Shortly thereafter, the German nurse disappeared and an equally strict English governess took her place. Apparently our parents had discovered that Sam and I were growing up speaking a kind of pidgin German.

At that age we took most of our meals in the kitchen with cook and nanny, a welcome relief from the rule of "seen and not heard" which prevailed in the dining room. However, another inflexible rule was "eat every bite on your plate!" I can still feel the hardness of the kitchen chair on my small behind after two hours of staring at a plateful of cold, slimy beets or shriveled calves' liver. I can also remember the sharp slap of a hair brush on the same part of my anatomy, always administered by the nurse. This weapon of punishment was reserved for my sister and me, while my brothers had to face a leather belt, wielded by Dad—though I suspect this was threatened more often than applied.

My earliest memory of myself as a child is of a painfully shy and skinny little girl with long dark braids, big freckles and braces on my teeth. I might not have been so acutely aware of my appearance if my brothers and sister had resembled me. But all four were blond and adorable. I knew I was the ugly duckling as I stood in the background while visitors exclaimed over Sam's irresistible smile, Tap's Norse-god profile, Frannie's honey-golden hair, Larry's mass of blond curls. How well I remember those tactless debates over whom I might be a throwback to, since Dad was a handsome blond, and Mother a beautiful redhead!

And so I grew older, always deeply anxious to please my parents, but at the same time convinced that I was failing to do so. I particularly remember creeping part way down the stairs one evening, long after we children had been put to bed, wishing I could be with Mom and Dad as I watched them sit together in the living room. I listened to snatches of their conversation—they were worried about Tap's temper tantrums, Sam's behavior at school. "Well," Dad sighed, "at least we can count on Tay—she's the Rock of Gibraltar." Mother nodded in agreement, and I crept back to bed feeling even more deeply unloved. They didn't have to care about me if I was a rock!

Doubtless it was seeing Frannie, so mature and poised in her bridal costume, that prompted these thoughts of the past. Or maybe it was our whole family being together again, in that sweltering little Florida church. But as these and a thousand other memories whirled through my head, I was startled to discover that it was the unhappy times— the loneliness, the hurts, the constant sense of inadequacy— that stood out from my childhood. The fun-filled family hours, the laughter, the companionship, why hadn't they mattered more?

From my teenage years there were happier memories. It was then I discovered I could gain my parents' enthusiastic approval by becoming a straight A student. I gained acceptance from my brothers too for being a strong tennis player, a "pretty good" deck hand on the sailboat, and not bad with a baseball bat. (I was their prize switch-hitter.)

I decided then that if I could do well enough at enough things, my deep-down sense of insecurity would gradually go away. Dad was delighted when I became interested in politics and international affairs. I looked forward to visiting with his guests then; rather than hiding in a corner, I would join in the discussions, holding my own as I continued to read voraciously and study hard. I often told myself that I was feeling more confident with every small achievement, and I particularly sensed Mother's and Dad's gratification when I graduated from my private school at the head of the class, and president of the student body as well.

My four years at Smith College were happier still. For the first time in my life I was free from being the "responsible eldest," free to choose my friends and activities. It was a delight just to lie in the sun hour after hour in order to compare tans, or sit and gossip in our rooms— wastes of time that weren't usually tolerated at home. I treasured long bike rides on beautiful spring days instead of feeling the compulsion to engage in competitive sports.

But at Smith too it was the desire for other people's approval which dictated much of what I did. I remembered endless long evenings at the local taverns, trying to appear engrossed in silly conversations while I struggled to get to the bottom of a glass of beer. I giggled dutifully over jokes, the point of which I utterly failed to grasp, and made re-peated unsuccessful efforts to learn to smoke. Night after night I'd go with "the crowd" to a popular seafood diner, although I hated shellfish or seafood of any kind. So much, in fact, of my life at college was governed by what I thought other people expected, that if anyone had said, "Will the real Tay Pryor please stand up," no one would have done so!

Lowell and I often wondered why our paths did not cross until Christmas vacation of my senior year at college. Our parents had been good friends from the time I was born, and Dad and Lowell Thomas Senior, already well-known as a newscaster, author and traveler, had many interests and friends in common. Mother and Dad spent occasional weekends at the Thomases' country farm in Pawling, New York, a short drive from Greenwich, and I remember Low-ell's parents visiting us once in the early forties. Lowell was a student at nearby Dartmouth College when I was at Smith, but his weekend dating took him to Bennington while I usually headed for Yale or Harvard. He even had a business meeting with my father once, to ask about pro-cedures for transporting a specially-equipped jeep to the Middle East.

I could still picture vividly every detail of the evening we met, and feel the excitement of the Christmastime at-mosphere. The house was filled with the fragrance of ever-green; pine boughs and holly were everywhere and a giant, brightly lit Christmas tree already stood in the center of the living room. A small pile of presents lay beneath the branches, but it was easy to guess from the flurry of secretive activity in several bedrooms designated "off-limits," that the pile would soon grow into a mountain.

In my bedroom that evening I could hear cheery voices as our guests arrived, and I hurried down the oak-paneled stairway to join in the welcome. Lowell was standing slightly apart from the four parents, a striking athletic figure, his sandy hair gleaming under the hall chandelier. He turned to watch me as I came nearer, and when I looked into his handsome, deeply tanned face and intense blue eyes, I knew beyond doubt in that instant that I had met the man I would eventually marry.

Lowell told me later that he wasn't sure why he allowed himself to be "dragged along" that night. He did not know I would be there, but he had a vague curiosity about this family he had heard led such an unconventional life. He remembered his father commenting on "that unusual Pryor family who go everywhere on motorcycles or in little airplanes." He felt awkward standing in the hall with the four older people, and when he heard footsteps on the stairs he looked up to see a tall thin girl with long dark hair, wearing a dress that was his favorite color green. He said he too knew at that instant that he had found "the one."

We talked together for every moment of the visit, completely oblivious to the presence of anyone else. I was attracted to a sense of strong character behind those blue eyes, not the cocky sureness which I'd encountered so often on college dates, but a quiet confidence of which he seemed to be totally unaware.

Although Lowell was an only child and I part of a large family, much of the rest of our backgrounds was amazingly similar. He, too, had been brought up by strict, concerned parents, who, like my own, were strong doers and achievers. They, also, were constant travelers, and when at home held open house to a wide assortment of fascinating people.

His father had planned for Lowell to follow in his footsteps at a very young age. Each day after elementary school, for example, Lowell had to make an oral report on all that had gone on of interest—a kind of early training for public speaking. As he grew older, he took on a variety of carefully planned summer experiences, beginning with a local ditch-digging job at fourteen, going on a Navy good-will cruise around South America as assistant to a movie cameraman at fifteen, and the following year joining a mountaineering expedition to Alaska.

World War II was an unforeseen interruption, and Lowell enlisted on his own initiative in the Army Air Corps. Those flying years were the happiest of his youth. He had discovered a talent of his very own, and if his career had not already been taken for granted, he might well have remained in the Air Force, or perhaps gone on into commercial aviation.

Instead, as soon as the war was over, Lowell went back to Dartmouth, and began journeys to various parts of the world during his summer breaks. Before he graduated he was already launched on his pre-planned career: giving illustrated lectures from his travels, and at the time we met had already begun to earn a reputation on the lecture platform.

Lowell's winter speaking tour that year, and the plans he had already made for a summer of travel in the Middle East and Tibet, forced us into a rather unique pattern of courtship—mostly by mail. He did manage to come see me once at Smith that spring, dropping in at the local airfield in a small borrowed plane. While I naturally thought nothing of his method of travel, my friends were agog.

We were able to squeeze in a few short visits between my graduation and his departure for the summer—all-too-brief times, but filled with the knowledge of the deep love growing between us. We told no one of our decision to be married; typical of the pattern of our life together, then and ever since, my parents and the rest of the world first learned of our wedding plans through a message relayed via a Tibetan ham radio operator. The personal call to me was monitored by Walter Winchell and printed in his gossip column, and I had plenty of explaining to do! The message had simply been: "All is well here in Tibet, can hardly wait for you to be with me on our next trip."

Actually, neither of our families can have been very surprised over our "news," and both gave our plans their wholehearted approval. We had quite a time settling on a wedding date, however, because Lowell was frantically busy all winter with the writing of a book and production of a film on Tibet. It was finally agreed we would squeeze it into late May, between lecture dates and a second trip to Tibet, which would serve as our honeymoon.

Our wedding itself, on May 20, 1950, was in many ways symbolic of our lives to that point—the only child and the eldest daughter of two prominent families meant the biggest event of the social season, a large formal Episcopal Church ceremony followed by a home reception. The guest list of many hundreds read like "who's who," and photographers had a field day with the Governor of New York, the Attorney General of the United States, the Mayor of New York City, movie stars and celebrities from many fields. A Metropolitan Opera singer sang at the service, and our four parents, gracious and obviously relaxed in familiar roles, greeted and visited with their many friends at the reception.

Where were the bride and groom? Supremely happy, but on our own little private cloud. We felt strangely detached, as though we were puppets in the elaborate celebration. We were only occasionally aware of the presence of our own friends in the crush of the crowd, and felt like we were drifting through a beautiful dream.

The resounding chords of the wedding recessional, almost earsplitting within the walls of the small Florida chapel, reminded me that this was not Lowell's and my wedding now, but Frannie's and Bob's. I waited for them to get a good start up the aisle, then followed at a suitable distance. Between smiling rows of family and friends I walked, toward the blinding tropical sunshine beyond the door.

Little did I dream that I was actually walking into the blackest time of my life.

3.

The Fear with No Name

It was dark in the house when I opened my eyes; a glance at the luminescent bedside clock told me it was 2:10 a.m. I wondered what had waked me, and why I'd been having such a restless, nightmarish sleep.

An all-too-familiar sensation was rising from deep within me—I couldn't identify it, except that it had something to do with losing control of myself. I lay there trying for the hundredth time to analyze what was happening to me, but as usual I could not get beyond recognizing a feeling of

total inadequacy. Not the kind I'd always felt when faced
with particular situations, but an all-pervasive one which
left me feeling helpless to do anything at all. I thought about
waking Lowell to seek his comfort, but changed my mind
because he simply would not understand. He always was
baffled by what he called "female emotions," and he'd be
particularly puzzled if I tried to describe a sensation I
couldn't even name.

At last I slipped out of bed and went through the dimly
lit hall, past the rooms where two-year-old Anne and four-
month-old Dave were sleeping, to the bathroom. I turned
on the light and stared at myself in the miror. I looked normal enough—tired and thin maybe—that was nothing new.
But as I stood there steadying myself against the basin,
I continued to feel that sense of overwhelming helplessness.
It had been happening more and more often, this feeling
that struck without warning—but this was the first time it
had waked me out of sleep.

Within a few moments the familiar waves of anxiety were
sweeping over me. I began to tremble in every muscle of my
body until I was drenched with perspiration, even though
in my thin nightgown I felt chilly. I opened the wall cabinet, reached for the sleeping pill bottle and gulped one
down, in spite of the fact that I had already taken one when
I went to bed that night. The pill seemed to help, but it was
a long while before I fell asleep again.

The next morning I felt groggy and tired but otherwise
all right. Whatever it was that had hit me the night before
had disappeared as usual as quickly as it had come. I
couldn't forget the experience, however, and I went through
the motions of daily life during the week that followed
wrapped in a kind of cocoon of introspection. It had happened for the first time, as near as I could recall, a couple
of years before, shortly after Anne was born in 1955. I could
make no sense of it; I had never thought much about my
inner life anyway. Mother and Dad had always been firm
about ignoring emotions, about living "on the outside of

ourselves" where there was no room for bad feelings of any kind.

A week after this nighttime experience, Lowell and I were watching a football game on television with the Thomas Seniors in their living room. We had just finished a meal that was perfectly ordinary, except for the effect it had had on me. I had refused a bowl of beets that was being passed, and my father-in-law inquired why. Instead of answering truthfully that I detested beets (I still held those long hours on the kitchen chair against them), I made some apologetic remark about preferring other vegetables more—peas, for example. I knew it was a lame excuse, but I was totally unprepared for the lecture that followed on the evils of peas: unhealthy, full of starch. L. T. Senior then launched into a discussion of certain other foods, especially a particular soft drink (my favorite) which had been demonstrated to remove the paint off a car.

No one else seemed in any way upset by the conversation, but when we finally left the table I felt like a squashed bug on a hard pavement. The TV helped—everyone had to be silent, and the tumult that had raged inside me was quieting down. Then without warning that feeling of self-control ebbing away was back, more terrifying than ever. The trembling started too, this time in front of other people. I hastily excused myself and fled to the bedroom where we'd put Anne and Dave down for the night.

As I leaned against the closed door I realized that something was really wrong with me, and that I needed some kind of professional help as fast as possible. But where to find it? Our own home was in Princeton, New Jersey, but as we spent most weekends, all holidays, and the summer months, either with the Thomases in Pawling or the Pryors in Greenwich, I hardly felt part of the community. Other than the pediatrician, I didn't feel I could approach a doctor there. And since we had never attended the Episcopal Church in Princeton, I could hardly go there for help. We had friends, of course, in New Jersey, but I was acutely aware of a barrier to some kinds of communication, in 1957—a stone wall dividing what was "okay" to talk about and what was taboo. I sensed that mental anguish was something one simply did not mention.

I felt more and more alone, there in the room with my two sleeping children, as I tried to think of someone to turn to. And then I remembered meeting a close friend and neighbor of the Thomases here in Pawling, Dr. Norman Vincent Peale. Dr. Peale, I knew, had a nationwide reputation for counseling people in trouble—and that included me for sure.

Normally I would never have had the courage to approach such an eminent person who was almost a total stranger, but desperation made me look up his phone number and set up an appointment—not of course in Pawling where my abnormal condition might become known, but at his office at Marble Collegiate Church in New York City.

To my amazement and relief, Dr. Peale showed no surprise whatsoever as I described my symptoms to him, sitting in a comfortable leather chair in his office the following week. In fact he nodded several times, as if this were the most familiar situation in the world. He agreed that counseling was called for; because of his close relationship with my in-laws he thought he would not be the proper person, but made arrangements that very day for me to see a therapist at the American Foundation for Religion and Psychiatry, sponsored by his church.

The person to whom he referred me was Dr. Herman Barbery, a gentle grandfatherly man with a twinkle in his eye and a quick warm smile. Again I described my mysterious condition, feeling comfort just from the fact that for the first time in my life I was putting some of my deep-down anxiety into words. I felt even better, as though some tremendous burden had been lifted, when, instead of looking bewildered and alarmed, he too nodded his head in understanding. "What you are experiencing is a very common loss of confidence," he said, "though it's a little unusual in a woman of thirty. Generally it hits men and women in their late forties or fifties."

I scarcely heard the rest of what he said. Just the fact that my problem had a name, that it was known and treatable, was such good news I wanted to weep with relief. Dr. Barbery—he was a clergyman as well as a psychologist—set up a series of weekly appointments with me, "to discover" as he gently put it, "just what is causing your upheaval." He also added that I could reach him by phone any time of the day or night. As I got up to go, he cautioned that for a while the problem might seem to get worse instead of better, as we stirred up deep-buried feelings. "Hang in there, and you'll find your way through to your real, whole self."

I had never realized just how out of touch with that self I was until, week by week, the doctor and I began peeling back the layers of superimposed attitudes and expectations. As he had predicted, the frightening, monstrous feeling of helplessness returned, sometimes taking over my life so completely that I could barely face even the most normal routines. It wasn't so bad within the four walls of our house, supported by Lowell (he was still puzzled but eager to help) and kept busy with two loving and deeply loved children. However, the moment I had to leave that base of security, I'd fall apart.

Going to the supermarket, once a simple and even pleasant change from chores at home, now became a giant test of my efforts to hold myself together. There was something about the shelves towering all about me jammed with items requiring decisions that triggered panic. I often grabbed the first can or box within reach just to get through the ordeal as fast as possible. And then there were the people shopping around me, all looking so confident and happy. I dreaded running into friends and felt like a fugitive as I peeked around corners to see if the way was clear.

The worst moment always awaited me at the end, at the check-out counter. I sensed that the checker disapproved of my choices as she grabbed my purchases from the cart and banged the keys of the register. One check-out clerk, an older woman whose hair, like my mother's, was worn in a bun at the back of her head, rang up a can of fruit and then said disdainfully, "Dearie, didn't you see such-and-such a brand on sale for five cents less?" It was all I could do to keep from running from the store, leaving my groceries behind.

Even more terrifying than the supermarket was the weekly train ride to New York, bearable at all only because it was taking me to my helper. (I literally counted the hours until my next appointment.) As I took my seat I felt all eyes on me and was sure they could see that I was going to visit a psychologist. I had made all sorts of excuses to my friends about these regular trips—I knew of no one else who had such problems. Everyone around me seemed completely in control of their lives except me.

The most frightening part of the train ride, however, was the approach of the blue-uniformed conductor, striding briskly down the aisle collecting and punching tickets. I lived in terror that I might have the wrong one; once, when I couldn't find it in my purse, he gruffly told me please to be ready for him the next time.

My fear of the conductor and the sense of being surrounded by unsympathetic passengers often triggered the familiar anxiety reaction. It would build up and up until I knew I had to run, to flee to a place away from people. The ladies' room on the train was usually filthy so I often spent the remainder of my ride standing in the wildly bucking connecting platform between cars, clinging to a handhold, staring out the window.

This same sense of panic, a desperate desire to flee from a crowded, seemingly threatening situation, took hold of me in theaters, at concerts and plays. No matter how entertaining the program, I could not fight down the panicky sense of being trapped, and so I insisted on an aisle seat, or, if that was impossible, developed a technique of starting a coughing fit so that I could excuse myself and dash for the door.

It didn't always take a group of strangers to start my panic, either. Sometimes, talking to a friend, I could feel myself begin to tremble, and would wonder in agony if it showed. It was particularly difficult if I was holding something—I would have to set a glass down, or refrain from picking up a desperately wanted cup of coffee.

The person who held me together throughout these constant ordeals was Dr. Barbery, who was always available, always ready to reassure me that my miserable experiences were a very normal part of this particular syndrome. "Relax and simply let these swells of anxiety flow over you," he'd say. "Nothing will happen. People won't notice as much as you think they do." One of the biggest discoveries of my life was the day I actually did this—sitting on a bench in crowded Grand Central Station.

I had just left the doctor, and felt the usual higher level of confidence which followed my sessions. However, fear began mounting as the crowd near the train gate increased. For a moment I was tempted to run again. Then I remembered Dr. Barbery's words and I thought, why not just sit here and let these awful feelings have their way. If I did begin to shake or sweat, this milling mob probably wouldn't notice, or at the most they'd think I was physically sick. There'd be no shame involved in that! And so I stayed on the hard bench, squeezed between two portly suburban matrons, simply letting go—wave after wave of anxiety pouring out from deep within. Nothing more than that happened, except for a rapidly beating heart (which no one could see) and a flushed face (not abnormal in that heat). No one even looked at me; in fact as I studied faces about me, each seemed locked in a very private world. Gradually I calmed down, breathing more easily. I had just conquered Mt. Everest!

I made other helpful discoveries in the sessions with my

counselor. In our talks together we first discussed my current life, looking for factors which might be contributing to my emotional problems. Being the mother of two small children certainly represented a tremendous change and challenge for me. I worried about them constantly, picturing to myself all the terrible things that might happen to them. There were powerful pluses to counteract these negatives, however. I loved being a mother more than anything else in the world, and I felt an uncharacteristic self-confidence in that role, despite my constant fretting, because as the oldest of five children I'd had plenty of practice.

The other pressure on me was Lowell's frequent absence from home. He continued to work on travel movies for his lectures and for television specials, journeying into out-of-the-way places for three or four months at a stretch. On the other hand, when Lowell was at home, although he never fully understood the difficulty I was facing, he gave me his fullest support. He was always willing to leave a concert or movie in the middle if I simply couldn't stand being squeezed in among people another moment, always demonstrative of his love and acceptance.

It became clear to me before very long that the good aspects of my life at the moment far outweighed the negative ones. It was time to look for the real reasons behind my anxiety. I didn't have far to go, because it was immediately obvious that my new relationship with two strong-willed, high-achieving parents-in-law was evoking childhood problems I'd never come to grips with. Just as I'd felt I was forever disappointing my own mother and father, so now I was falling into the same pattern with an additional set of parents. Every well-meant suggestion about child care, cooking, household management, I took as a condemnation of an already deeply insecure self.

As luck would have it, my mother-in-law was one of those efficient, skillful, utterly capable women who made me feel inadequate just by entering a room. In fact she didn't have to be there: the first time I tried to pack a suitcase for Lowell he told me rather pityingly that his mother had taught him the right way to fold a jacket, the order in which shirts, socks, ties and so on down to the smallest item should be placed, and that he would prefer to pack his own bag.

Mother Fran, as I called her, was an expert hostess, able to entertain any number of people in a seemingly effortless and flawless manner, even on a moment's notice. I was so impressed with her ability that it took me months to find the courage to invite them to our home for a meal. Unfortunately I aimed too high, a Thanksgiving dinner. Of course I was in a dither for days beforehand although the two of them were to be our only guests. When the big day finally came, I was not only exhausted, but I did every possible thing wrong. The turkey that Lowell carved was pink, the stuffing cold, the rice almost raw, and the brussels sprouts an unidentifiable pulpy glob. Needless to say, many months went by before I found the courage to try again.

Just talking with Dr. Barbery about the complexity of family relationships, discovering the reasons behind actions and attitudes, learning to see our four parents as individuals with problems of their own, was a help in itself. As the months went by he also encouraged me to look at my own self as a bright, talented person with strengths as well as weaknesses. "You can't possibly please everybody all the time, or even half of it," he said over and over. "You are first responsible for one person—yourself. Ask yourself what do *you* want, what do *you* feel and think"—questions I had never even considered before.

As I did consider them, week in and week out for almost a three-year period, I learned a lot about my feelings and how to handle them. Back in my earliest years, when we played the "Jungle Path" game, we were taught that fear did not exist. It did exist, in me, but because Dad said it didn't I tried to force it down, to bury it, to deny it—always failing, always feeling like a traitor. With the guidance of Dr. Barbery I was finally able to acknowledge many of my fears, to admit to them and talk about them freely, seeing now that there was nothing so criminal about feeling this way. With increased understanding I found it easier to handle my present-day life. Every time I stayed to the end of a movie I counted it as a major triumph, and facing up to an authority figure without flinching was another step taken.

But I was far from being a secure person when in 1960 Lowell and I moved away from the New York area. For a long time Lowell had been unhappy with the pressures of the television documentary world. He hated commuting to New York City, hated flying our small plane along the crowded air corridors of the East Coast. Above all he longed to find a place where he could film and write about the wilderness without leaving his family for such long stretches. For months we'd pored over atlases, always arriving at the same answer.

Alaska.

Lowell had been to Alaska many times and loved it already; I'd had only one brief visit, but knew I could love it too. It would mean a tremendous relocation, leaving the part of the country where we'd lived all our lives, saying goodbye to family and friends and—especially hard for me just now—Dr. Barbery. But in Alaska Lowell would find the camping, skiing and outdoor life he loved, Anne and Dave would grow up in the kind of environment we'd always wanted for them, together the four of us would have a chance to help build a new state from a raw frontier.

It was a challenge too great to resist, and if we were going the best time was now. Anne was five, next year she'd be starting school. And so in the summer of 1960 we packed up everything we owned and headed West.

4.

Why Don't You Follow Me?

Why did I ever think Alaska is just a land of snow and ice, I thought, as I stared down at the evergreen forest beneath our small plane. There seemed no end, hardly even a break in the endless wilderness of trees. Directly below, as I kept glancing down from the map on my lap, the broad, brown Yukon River twisted its way through the forest land between wide gravel bars. Good landing places, I thought, as I glanced apprehensively toward the menacing black line of thunderheads hanging low over the hills to our right.

"Dear, do you think those storms are heading our way?" I turned to Lowell with an anxious look. "Just building up over high land," he said, scarcely glancing up from his computations on our fuel consumption. What a competent flyer, I thought, as I watched his hand resting gently on the controls, his occasional sharp glances at the instrument panel, or out the windows. But then he had always had that look of confidence when behind the wheel of an airplane. He seemed completely at home again, happy to be flying over the wilderness of Alaska rather than fighting the busy airways over New York.

How I wished I felt the same! At that moment the plane hit an air pocket, bouncing us sharply. I grabbed my armrest, then turned quickly and looked at the children, squeezed together between our camping gear in the back seat. Completely at home, too, I thought, with relief. Anne had made her first flight in our little plane when she was six weeks old, and as soon as Dave was born he came right along, too. Veteran flyers now at five and three, they might just as well be in a car going to the local supermarket. Their heads together, they were working intently on a new coloring book, oblivious to their surroundings.

"Hey, look!" Lowell shouted, as he banked the plane sharply. "Fire!" Crayons flew in all directions as the children scrambled for their windows. Lowell circled more tightly and then pushed the nose down steeply toward the small hillside below. I clung to my seat in alarm, feeling dizzy from the abrupt movements of the little plane. "Please, take it easy, dear," I murmured so that the children would not hear. "Take it easy yourself!" he reproached me.

The excited squeals from the back seat were too much— I had to glance out my window at the spiraling ground below. Gray streamers of smoke were rising from an almost perfect circle of small tongues of fire. It was easy to see the flames from our 200-foot altitude, and fascinating, in a ghoulish way, to watch them spread and grow larger before our eyes. A shrub or small tree would suddenly burst into flame, sparks and smoke erupting toward us.

"This is a new one all right. We'd better report it," and with microphone in hand, Lowell called Kotzebue radio. The kids hung over his shoulder, waiting eagerly for the reply to come over our speaker. "Roger, 43 Charlie, we have your report. Could you circle for a while longer to see if it's going to spread?" My fervent plea to forget the whole thing was drowned out by Dave's shouts of glee. Fires started by lightning in Alaska's vast wilderness were a constant concern in the state, and teams of men and planes played a dramatic role in attempts to combat them during the summer months each year.

And so we circled and circled, while I wrestled with my mounting anxiety. How odd I hadn't felt this way on our Flight to Adventure, I thought. And here we were, in the same plane, good old "Charlie," as we fondly called it. Various souvenirs from exotic parts of the world still hung from the fabric ceiling of the plane's interior, and my favorite prayer remained taped to the instrument panel. "The Lord be at thy side to bless and guide." The words still gave me that faint inexplicable sense of reassurance.

The back seat filled with two wiggling, excited little children was certainly a difference, however! I looked at Anne, dark-haired and pretty, with a lithe, muscular body inherited from her Dad. Intense, forceful and talkative—we should have named her for a mountain peak in Hunza, I thought with a smile. Dave was so opposite in many ways— blond and chubby, with a cherub's face and disposition.

I felt the usual intense feeling of love, as I watched them dart from window to window. Surely, I kept telling myself, this accounted for my newly developed nervousness about flying: now we had these two precious lives to protect. Yes, I was different, too. Even though I was sitting in my same old seat, maps on my lap, I had obviously changed in those painful years after our travels—for the better, I hoped, after all the time and patience Dr. Barbery had expended on me.

I glanced at Lowell, busy with the controls and the radio. He loved our new life here in every way, especially the out-of-doors living, well away from the urban existence we had both grown to dislike so much. His brisk, confident voice answered Kotzebue radio. "Roger, the fire is definitely spreading, we'll head on now," was his final report.

"Well," he told the jubilant kids, "they're sending out a plane with fire-fighters right away." I settled back with relief as the plane climbed back up to a higher altitude, and within a few minutes I spotted the dark blue of the Chukchi Sea far ahead of the plane—my first glimpse of these far northern waters.

Our destination that day was the tiny Eskimo village of Point Hope. It was an easy place to locate—on my map of Alaska I simply selected the finger of land (Point Hope's Eskimo name means index finger) that sticks the farthest out into the Chukchi Sea toward Siberia. The village itself, I saw as Lowell brought Charlie in for a landing, was a handful of small weatherbeaten box-like buildings built on the flat sand, home to about 350 people. Whoever named it Hope must either have been in highly desperate circumstances, or else expected to find the elusive Northwest Passage just around the corner.

Point Hope was celebrating the 75th anniversary of the founding of the first Arctic Coast Episcopal mission, and in true warm Eskimo hospitable fashion, the residents had extended an open invitation to take part in their festivities. About one hundred Alaskans were expected, along with a dozen guests from the "Lower 48." Dignitaries were to be Alaska's Episcopal Bishop William Gordon, and the state's governor, William Egan.

Cooking for several hundred people is no big deal in a native village; the trick is for the visitor to learn to eat walrus meat, whale blubber and seal oil-and-berry "ice cream." Fortunately for our children and other picky eaters, Bishop Gordon had promised to supplement the menu by flying in crates of oranges and cans of ham.

Providing accommodations was no problem for the villagers, either: they simply opened their long-unused

two-story rectory building and the more modern one-floor
schoolhouse, suggesting that visitors bring their sleeping
bags. In fact, the only reason more Alaskans didn't head for
Point Hope and the festivities was the almost total lack of
access. One simply had to fly, there was no scheduled airline
service, and the gravel airstrip was barely big enough for a
chartered DC-3.

We had come a day ahead of the crowd, and we parked
Charlie beside a sign that informed us exactly where we
were. One marker on the post pointed east with the information that New York was 4,200 miles away. Another, indicat-
ing north, said "Barrow 325 miles," and the third one aimed
at Siberia, just 200 miles to the west! Now that we knew
precisely where we were, we looked about us, and loved
what we saw. I had not expected an Arctic coast setting so
serenely beautiful, under this cloudless blue sky, with a
70-degree temperature and no wind.

We decided to pitch the family tent on the tundra behind
the village. Our carpeting was of mosses, lichens and grasses,
and a mass of exquisite miniature wild flowers. How could
something so fragile grow at this northern latitude I wondered, as I touched a pink and white orchid-shaped blossom
the size of my thumbnail. I felt an actual physical hurt inside me whenever I had to step on them—they must have
struggled so to survive here.

The children and I spent the afternoon walking on the
beach, wondering at the ice floes on the distant horizon, and
the sand dunes which looked as though they might be con-
cealing the remains of long-past settlements. Archeologists
believe that Point Hope may be the oldest presently inhabited site in Alaska. We visited the few remaining traditional sod homes, built half underground for warmth,
walked past wooden racks covered by strips of seal and
whale meat drying in the sun, and wandered among the old
graves of the cemetery, enclosed by a fence of eight-foot-
high whale jaw bones. Hunting whales is a centuries-old
tradition among these people, and whale meat the mainstay

of their diet. When we finally crawled into our sleeping bags that night we were convinced that Point Hope was one of the loveliest summer sea resorts on earth.

The rude awakening came shortly after midnight when the wind began to blow—a strong, icy one straight from the North Pole. By morning we were hanging on to the tent poles to keep the tent from blowing down, our teeth chattering in the cold. We hastily decided to abandon our private residence and staked our claim to a small storeroom in the rectory. We were now seeing Point Hope under much more normal weather conditions—the pack ice just offshore, blown landward by a freezing gale, low clouds and thick fog.

That day, between numerous trips to greet arriving visitors, the villagers and guests kept warm by taking part in traditional foot races and an Eskimo "blanket" toss with walrus hides. Those who, like me, were too shy to participate, gradually turned to blocks of ice. We thawed out quickly, however, at the Eskimo "potlatch" held indoors that evening. After the communal dinner, the Eskimos sang and danced to the accompaniment of drums, their beaming faces and rollicking laughter creating an atmosphere of warmth and friendliness. I wondered, as I snuggled into my sleeping bag that night, how people living in such a harsh environment could be so cheerful and generous.

Next morning we all squeezed into St. Thomas' Church for a communion service. *Squeezed* is definitely the word because two hundred of us, wearing a variety of heavy jackets and native parkas, jammed onto narrow wood benches designed to seat half that number. The plain wood walls and bare floor of the little church were offset by exquisite beadwork hangings on the altar and a white polar bear rug lying before it. And I noticed beaded moccasins peeking from beneath the lay reader's traditional white robes.

As I listened to Bishop Gordon read the words of the prayers I had heard so often in my childhood, I marveled that they could be the same in a setting so different. When

I was a youngster, we sat on red velvet cushions in a pew reserved just for our family each Sunday. The massive stone walls of the cathedral-like church in Greenwich, the lofty oak rafters far over my head, and the ornate hanging lights had filled me with awe. I never dared squirm during the long service, much less sing aloud with joyful abandon as these people around me were doing now. The stained-glass windows in Greenwich were beautiful, especially the one over the distant altar, of Jesus holding a lamb in His arms. There'd been times when I had a wild longing to be picked up and held like that lamb, but He was so far away.

My religious upbringing had been confined within those rigid stone walls to an hour each week, along with brief, painful Sunday school classes, when we were required to stand and recite prayers or the Ten Commandments. My confirmation memories were of a white veil, a seemingly endless aisle to negotiate, and a service of even more than usually awesome pageantry. After our marriage in 1950 (that same aisle seemed just as long), Lowell and I seldom attended church at all.

As I listened to Bishop Gordon now, his voice betraying his North Carolina background, I thought about the camaraderie which had grown between Lowell and Alaska's "Flying Bishop" as Lowell began work on a film for the Diocese of Alaska. Theirs was an instant friendship, kindled while "fire-potting" their airplane engines in the sub-zero Arctic winter, refueling their planes from gas drums in the numbing cold, flying together between isolated Indian and Eskimo village missions. Bishop Gordon was on the go almost every day of the year—baptizing, confirming, marrying, counseling, sharing the lives of his far-flung flock. Although his huge district included the cities and towns of southeastern and south central Alaska, I suspected the best part of the job to him was flying his Cessna 180 to minister to the peoples of the far north.

Bishop Gordon's prayers were followed by the boisterous singing of a communion hymn, visitors in English, Eskimos in their native language. I watched the faces of the villagers as they went to and from the altar for communion—many of the women carrying babies under their fur-lined parkas. All were smiling, but there was something more, a kind of radiant joy, a look of deep peace and inner serenity in their eyes. How was such calm possible, I wondered as I listened to the Arctic gale howling outside the church. I was surprised that these women would bring tiny babies out in such weather, and I wondered if they worried about their older children playing out of doors. We could occasionally hear their shouts and laughter as they romped just beyond the church windows. I was tense with concern over our own two who had begged to stay outside with the other youngsters. Were they warm enough? Were they wearing their caps and mittens as they had been told?

I knew, too, that these Eskimo men and women faced an insecure livelihood, dependent on the whale catch each spring, and on fishing, hunting and berry-picking—subsistence living which could fluctuate wildly from one year to the next. It was a life of physical danger too, as they pitted their skills against the most savage elements of nature. Staring at their serene faces my sense of wonder grew—I wanted to find out what their secret was and share it with them!

I could certainly have used some of that serenity during the flight home that day. The weather continued bad—the wind had died down, but it was raining and patches of fog hung low along the coastline. I hated taking off under such conditions and gripped the edge of my seat as I watched the ground fall away beneath us. There was a 300-foot ceiling of thick clouds above the wispy patches of ground fog, so we had to fly low, almost skimming the beaches, Bishop Gordon flying his small plane just ahead of us.

When it was time to turn inland, down the wooded Kobuk River valley and then across the Hog River hills, the visibility worsened. I was frantic—after all, the shoreline was relatively flat but now we were heading for higher ground, with clouds threatening to close down on us at any moment. It was then that the bishop called us via radio: "Four-three Charlie, why don't you follow me?" Lowell quickly acknowledged in the affirmative, knowing that the church leader had flown this route regularly for many years. He closed in behind the other plane, almost flying formation, keeping in constant radio contact.

I was a nervous wreck. Normally I would have been pleading with Lowell to turn back because of the poor flying conditions, but with our much admired and respected bishop leading the way, I could only bite my lip and clutch the armrest. Worst of all, I detected a certain smug look on Lowell's face. He knew the predicament I was in and was thoroughly enjoying it!

It was helpful to follow the bishop's plane, I had to admit: it was reassuring to know that he was familiar with every twist and turn of the river and with the shape and height of all the hills around us. Below us the wooded slopes were horrifyingly close; I kept my eyes riveted on the bishop's plane instead, although generally all that was visible among the gray clouds was the bright red rotating light on the tail. I focused on that, and my total faith in the bishop and his knowledge of the terrain. What a wonderful thing it was, I thought, to have something so tangible on which to pin my trust . . .

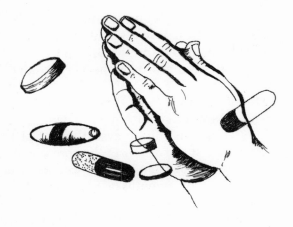

5.

A Pill to Sleep By

I stood at the edge of our high bluff land, our own little stake in Alaska, recently purchased after renting another house in the neighborhood for a year. The north wind was cool as always, even in midsummer. I was looking toward a distant pyramid of white—Mt. McKinley, over 20,000 feet high, 140 miles due north. When the clouds so frequently covering it moved aside, I always had to take time to admire this majestic natural monument, highest in North America. There was something particularly awe-inspiring about its aloneness

—even more than the massive snow-covered peaks of the Alaska Range to my left.

These mountains were like a great mound of stiff-whipped cream the year around, several of the peaks rising to twelve and thirteen thousand feet. When we first moved there, I often mistook them for a bank of boiling white clouds. There was something almost mystical to me about them because they were still volcanically alive. An eruption had occurred just five years before, spewing ash over the very ground I was standing upon.

The Chugach Mountains, to my right, were more similar to those I'd known in New England but on a far grander scale—the way this state seemed to do everything. Just beyond the city of Anchorage they rose abruptly from sea level to 10,000 feet. The upper slopes, craggy and treeless, were covered with snow almost ten months a year. The lower elevations were a constantly changing pattern of summer green, russet autumn tones, winter white. They were at their glorious best during the coldest months when the sun was low in the sky, sometimes turning the snow brilliant pink against a deep blue sky.

If I ever became homesick for Long Island Sound, I could simply shift my gaze to the deep fjord-like waters of Turnagain Arm, not far from where I stood. It was on his final voyage, just before his untimely death in Hawaii, that Captain Cook sailed up this narrow waterway, believing he had discovered the long-sought Northwest Passage. But his small ship could make no headway against the enormous tides (in fact the inlet eventually ends in a glacier). A young seaman named William Bligh—later to become famous as captain of *The Bounty*—was historian for the journey. "We turn again," he wrote sadly in his journal, and Turnagain Arm had its name.

The color of the water often changed as I watched it from brown to green to blue, and in midwinter the surface was choked with great blocks of sea ice. A far cry from the placid millpond-like Sound of my childhood days, but nonetheless the smell of salt and seaweed and rotting shellfish, the mewing of seagulls overhead, all helped bridge that enormous distance to my eastern home.

What a spectacular setting for a city, I thought as I turned my eyes toward the small area of flat ground at the foot of the Chugach range. The eighteen and twenty-story concrete and glass "skyscrapers" of the downtown area rose in sharp contrast to their natural surroundings. Certainly nothing like the New York City skyline, but surprisingly urban for this wilderness setting. I definitely preferred looking at Anchorage from this vantage point, to driving through the crowded streets vainly looking for a parking space.

When we first moved to Anchorage, a little over a year before, we had three choices of where to live: far out on the wooded slopes of the mountains, isolated and reached by almost impassable roads; in quiet, tree-lined residential areas squeezed between downtown business blocks, where the earliest settlers still owned modest homes; or in the Turnagain-by-the-Sea, Alaska's first real suburb, complete with paved streets, street lights, manicured lawns and handsome fifty- to hundred-thousand-dollar homes. In fact Turnagain closely resembled the New Jersey area we had just left, and while old-timers beamed with delight over their magnificent new development, it wasn't what we'd expected of Alaska, and Lowell was disappointed.

I'd had a nagging concern that he'd like nothing better than a small log cabin perched high on a hilltop far from town. I liked that part of the picture, but not the thought of the isolation the children and I would face while Lowell was off traveling. Fortunately for the peace of our household, we stumbled upon a little corner of "semi-wilderness" at the very southern edge of the Turnagain suburb. Maybe the developers had run out of money by the time they had gone that far, but what a great break, I thought, that their bulldozers had not found these giant evergreens. I looked at the trees on the bluff about me: many were over fifty feet high, unusual for this area of poor soils. There were also tall stands of aspen and birch mingling with the stately pines. Closer to the ground I recognized wild red currant bushes, the tall fuchsia fireweed, the thorny devil's club plants, and the tiny wild dogwood. My special joy, however, was to discover that our two acres of woods harbored a thick carpet of delicious wild cranberries. I looked forward to sending cranberry bread and cranberry relish as Christmas presents to "outside" members of our family that winter.

As I wandered among the clumps of wild growth, carefully avoiding the devil's club, I found an odd-looking, jagged depression, a drop in the surface of the ground, about three feet in width. It must be an old stream bed, I guessed. Then I noticed several good-sized trees growing from the middle of the little ravine. It would have to be a very ancient stream bed indeed—surely it should have filled in by now? A few yards farther I came across two more of the strange trenches. They ran parallel to each other, and all ran parallel to the bluff. . . . Then, I reflected, water runoff could not be the cause either. We had been told that the Anchorage area was subject to earthquakes—always mild, no cause for alarm. I had heard of fissures caused by quakes, but surely the gentle tremors described to us could not affect the ground this drastically?

Dismissing the mystery, I turned and looked back at our long low farmhouse nestling in the woods behind me. We had painted it barn red, a touch of New England nostalgia in our permanent Alaskan home. Yes, it was permanent, it had to be, I thought as I headed towards the house. I had been so fed up with years of living out of suitcases, years of weekend and holiday commuting between our New Jersey home and our families in New York and Connecticut, that I'd told my new Alaskan friends only bulldozers could make me move again.

I walked around to the front door, waving to the children playing in the yard with some neighborhood friends. Inside the house a feeling of safety, of stability and security flooded over me. It was our lovely old early American furniture that did it, I thought, as I ran my hand over the velvet softness of the old pine cupboard in the hallway. The Sheraton sideboard in the living room, the Windsor chairs and Hepplewhite table, all given us by my family, spoke to me of continuity and certainty and a structured, dependable existence. It was funny I'd scarcely noticed them as a child; now I spent hours polishing the gleaming old wood with a special beeswax Dad had sent me.

I'd also developed a regular ritual for cleaning the beautiful silver we had received as wedding presents. (Much of it had been unpacked for the first time here in Alaska.) Spreading newspapers on the kitchen counter, I'd gather the pieces about me and rub them until they shone. They were like tangible evidence of the settled existence I hoped earnestly we'd achieved.

I felt a similar sensation of support when I looked out our kitchen window toward the twelve other homes along our dead-end dirt road, Chilligan Drive. It was a secluded neighborhood, the houses blending unobtrusively among the big trees. We were a close-knit group of families, drawn together by our love of the naturalness of our surroundings, rather than the formal gardens and immaculate lawns of the rest of Turnagain. Children brought us together too—at the moment the count was twenty-nine youngsters under sixteen years old! I felt a new sense of belonging, of sharing with friends after so many years of nomadic life.

Another new-found friend was our family doctor, Rod Wilson. Lowell had quickly discovered a kindred spirit in Rod—both loved to climb mountains and they often took off on short expeditions up nearby peaks. It was Rod who first confronted me, during a routine physical checkup, with one of the biggest challenges of my life.

After the examination he sat at his desk tapping a pencil, spending what seemed like ages going over my charts. Finally he pushed his chair back, took off his glasses, and said he was most concerned over my regular renewal of several sleeping prescriptions. My heart almost stopped as he went on to say he felt I must begin immediately to break what appeared to be a strong dependency. I suppose I had dreaded this ultimatum at every check-up time for years; now that I was faced with it, I was overwhelmed with terror.

I had always had problems with sleep, my fears and anxieties creating extra havoc at bedtime, and I started the regular use of sleeping pills when Lowell and I began our travels right after marriage. I found it particularly hard to get used to strange beds, odd hours and time changes, and therefore felt justified in using pills, always with a doctor's prescription, and never in excess of the number prescribed.

Then came the years of emotional upheaval in New Jersey which required the continued use of sleeping pills at night, as well as tranquilizers during the daytime. And now all the new adjustments to life in Alaska—where in summer bedtime found the sun still streaming through the windows! I knew I had become a regular "pill popper" and realized it was now an ingrained habit, but each time I'd try to cut down, some new crisis or problem would come along, and I'd decide to postpone the effort until a quieter interlude. After all, I needed the sleep in order to cope with whatever difficulty I was facing at the moment. Now I was stunned, almost crying. "Not now, Rod," I pleaded. "I'm just starting a new book project and I don't have enough energy as is!"

Rod, however, was adamant. He told me gently but firmly that he would help me work on it in a gradual way. I was to keep a chart and see him once a month to check on my progress. He put an arm around my shoulder as I went out the door. "I know you can do it," he said.

With Rod's encouragement, and the knowledge that he would not cut me off from drugs instantly, I decided to make a sincere effort. At home I dug up an unused calendar and chose symbols for the various potent and less potent pills I was using, deciding on an X for failure nights and large stars for success. I also decided to cut down on evening activities as much as possible, and try to keep early mornings open so that I could stay in bed longer if I hadn't slept.

This initial attempt was a flat failure—after one week my chart was covered with symbols and large black X's. Each evening I began worrying about the situation long before going to bed; by the time I was ready to turn in, those long-familiar waves of anxiety would be rising inside me. I'd start out without the usual aids; within an hour tension would have built up to the point that I'd realize I was facing a sleepless night. In the following wakeful hour, I'd worry about the exhaustion I'd feel the next day. Inevitably I'd capitulate and head for the medicine cabinet.

I decided then that I was going to need all the help I could get: the roots of my problem were undoubtedly deep since I could remember fighting insomnia even during college days. Again I could not turn to Lowell because he was one of those infuriating people who fell into a sound sleep the moment his head hit the pillow and never moved until the alarm went off next morning. He also abhorred all use of pills, disdaining even aspirin. And I did not want to return to Rod without a single success to report.

Who else was there? And then I thought of St. Mary's Episcopal Church. For years I'd had the nagging feeling that the children ought to be going to Sunday School; Dave's entering kindergarten this past fall had finally jarred me into action. After weeks of searching for a church I'd walked through the doors of St. Mary's and known instantly that I'd found it—a warm, friendly place with the same mixture of informality and enthusiasm we'd noticed at Point Hope.

And one of St. Mary's parishioners, Chuck Harris, had a reputation as an expert counselor. The rector at St. Mary's, Sandy Zabriskie, spoke to him about me, and even provided his study as a place where we could meet.

"Do you feel, Tay," Chuck asked as we sat in Sandy's book-lined office, "that you really need eight full hours of sleep every night?" When I answered with an emphatic "yes" he wanted to know why. "Well—so I'll be rested." "Have you ever tried short cat naps," he said, "or some exercise, on days when you haven't had enough sleep?" I could never relax enough to nap, I assured him, and exercise . . . wouldn't exercise simply compound my fatigue?

Chuck then asked me about my sleep habits when I was young. I remembered all too clearly the strong emphasis on "early to bed and at least nine hours of sleep"—another widely held belief of that era. We children were convinced that if we got less, we would be sick. When we reached our teens and were allowed to stay out late on weekends, we were always encouraged to sleep late the following morning.

"Did this habit change when you went off to college?" Chuck asked. "Oh no," I laughed, "I was the only girl in the dorm who went to bed at nine-thirty every night. The other girls thought I was crazy." In fact, I told him, my concern over lack of sleep began during that period, when I'd be forced to study late for exams.

Our first talk ended at this point, with Chuck suggesting I make the effort to do some walking (at that period in my life housework and chasing after children left me so exhausted I had little zest for physical exercise). "It's a great way to get rid of tension," he said. He added that there was no scientific evidence that people needed eight hours of sleep every night.

At our next meeting in the rector's study (I was deeply discouraged because my homemade chart still recorded nothing but failures), Chuck confronted me with a strange question: "How quickly do you go to sleep after taking a pill?" I thought a moment. "Within five or ten minutes." Chuck smiled. "You see, then, it's not the medicine itself that puts you to sleep, but the simple act of taking the pill. No medicine acts that fast." That was a revelation to me, something I had never thought about. He next asked me just what the pills symbolized to me, what reaction I felt toward them. That was difficult, and I had to think quite a while. "I suppose, comfort," I finally decided.

We then started probing back for my earliest memories of insomnia. I was surprised to realize that it had started long before my college years. Now that I tried, I could remember many miserable nights of sleeplessness during my childhood—of lying awake in my bed, surrounded by a dark and quiet home. Everyone was asleep but me, and the loneliness became frightening as the dark corners in the room moved closer and the old house creaked. I remembered looking out the window at the weird shadows cast by the street light, and, on moonlit nights, at the wildly waving black branches of the locust trees against the pale sky— threatening and snake-like in their motion.

I didn't know why I'd had such trouble falling asleep. Perhaps, Chuck suggested, because I was basically a night person and our parents put us all to bed exceptionally early. (They themselves were day people, always asleep by ten o'clock.) Whatever the reason, I desperately hated lying there all alone, and often ran through the bathroom to my parents' room for comfort.

"Mummie," I whispered, as I gently shook her awake. "What's wrong, dear?" she'd reply sleepily. My youngest brother and sister slept near our nanny, who dealt with their nighttime problems, while Sam and Tap shared a room at the far end of the hall and had each other to turn to. So Mother was stuck with me, and must have puzzled often over how to deal with such an overly imaginative child. Only years later did I realize, too, how tremendous was her own need, in her strenuous life, for an uninterrupted night's sleep. "Tay," she'd whisper at last in bafflement, "why don't you get the aspirin bottle from the medicine cabinet and put it on the table by your bed. If you really need it, take just one."

"What does that memory say to you?" Chuck asked gently.

I considered this for a few moments. Then a momentous realization hit me: "Why, of course, a pill symbolizes love to me!"

"Do you believe," Chuck went on, "that God loves you?"

"God loves everybody," I parried a little evasively.

"And 'everybody' has to include you?"

"Yes, I guess so."

And suddenly I found myself thinking of the tail light on Bishop Gordon's airplane, of the help and comfort I had drawn from that sight when everything else was hidden by clouds. What if I could find some tangible object, some physical symbol that could represent God's ever-present love for me, and hold it while going to sleep at night as a substitute for a pill?

With the help of further sessions in the following weeks I began to feel less afraid of sleepless nights. "So what!" I told myself—and I actually discovered that when I did feel tired, a brisk walk was helpful. Once I'd learned that I would not become deathly ill or fall apart from lack of sleep, the first bright stars of triumph began to appear on my chart. It was with great pride that I showed them to Rod Wilson each month, especially as the number rose from two to three, or even four, a week. Occasionally I retrogressed and felt badly about it, but Rod dismissed this as a normal part of the process. Almost a year went by before I achieved my first seven-star week—a cause for great celebration!

As I began to break the sleeping pill habit I was surprised to discover a number of pleasant side effects. Regardless of the amount of hours I'd slept, I felt more alert in the morning, it became easier to go back to sleep again at night if awakened, and, most exciting of all, I was discovering a deep sleep which I never remembered experiencing before. But the greatest change of all came in connection with the physical symbol that I substituted for the pill bottle.

My quest for this tangible object which could serve as a reminder of God's love took a number of weeks. I thought of and rejected a dozen ideas. Then one day while I was washing dishes at the sink I glanced up and noticed a small wooden plaque perched on the window sill. I had never seen it before and picked it up wondering how it had gotten there, and to whom it belonged. Praying hands were depicted in silver on a small rectangle of dark wood. Beneath them a metal scroll bore these words:

God grant me the serenity to accept the things I cannot
 change,
the courage to change the things I can,
and the wisdom to know the difference.

Amen

The little plaque fit snugly in my hand, the smooth wood cool to touch, and as I held it I realized that I had found my symbol. But where had it come from? Neither Anne nor Dave had seen it before, nor had Lowell, when I asked him later. We had no guests at the time, and it seemed for a while that it had literally dropped out of the sky. And then we remembered my "angel."

Lowell and I had never felt we could afford a cleaning lady, except during those times when I was working on a book. Then I'd usually get someone to come in and help out once or twice a week. Now, starting a manuscript on life in Alaska, I was desperate for a helping hand.

It didn't take long to discover that household help of any kind was a rarity in Anchorage. After much fruitless searching, I decided we'd simply have to put up with a dirty house until the project was finished. It was then I got a phone call from a young woman who said she was a friend of a neighbor. She was tired of working in an office and willing to help me out.

Not only was Edith's arrival exceptionally timely, she herself was a delight to have around. I had not forewarned her that we had six cats and a ferocious ninety-pound German Shepherd, but Edith thought the animals were great—she had once worked for a veterinarian. Instead of his usual frenzied barking and bared teeth when a stranger appeared, Bozie walked right up to Edith and licked her hand. She did not mind stepping over the cats as she vacuumed, and Lowell's work papers scattered all over the house did not disturb her in the least. In fact, we discovered that she was a skilled typist, and she gladly offered to help us with that chore, too.

Seemingly there was nothing that Edith could not do, or minded doing, with never a complaint and always a cheerful smile. It was only natural that I began to call her "my angel," and who knows, perhaps she really was. When the writing chore was finished she disappeared as suddenly as she had come. . . . Surely it was Edith who had left me the plaque as a parting gift.

And now that I had found my symbol, I clutched it in my hand each night as I lay down, drawing comfort from the solidity and firmness of it, as much as from the beautiful prayer inscribed on it. Just as chairs and tables and silverware spoke to me of permanence, so this little piece of wood began to speak to me of God, reassuring me in the darkness that He was there, near and strong and terribly real—if only I knew where to find Him.

6.

The Solid Ground

The wind was icy although it was the month of June—I felt it blowing right through me as I tried to handle the shovel with frozen fingers. I was determined to plant a vegetable and flower garden again this summer, although the one we'd put in last year, our first summer in our new home, had been a dismal failure. The cabbage never even headed and the ears of corn by the end of the growing season were the size usually served as hors d'oeuvres at cocktail parties. As

much as we loved our large trees, they did block out the
sunlight.

Wanda Mead, our nearest neighbor along the bluff, must
have a green thumb, I decided, as I tried to dig out a large
rock, one of many I'd encountered that afternoon. The Perry
Mead family had just built their new home next door to us—
one they had dreamed about and planned for five years.
Perry, Alaska's only neurosurgeon, was forced to spend most
of his time at the hospital but Wanda was always busy with
projects about their dream house. When the weather was
good she worked outdoors all day, hauling large stones to
create a rock garden, mixing cement herself to form a retain-
ing wall around some of her prize trees.

Whenever the five children could be corralled, Wanda put
them to work, too. Perry Junior, the oldest, a mature, good-
looking boy of twelve, was a top student as well as a promis-
ing skier, but also his mother's indispensable helper around
the house. When outdoors, he divided his time between lifting the heavier rocks and chasing after his two younger
brothers. Paul, an energetic three-year-old, had an almost
magical way of disappearing, to turn up a mile away within
minutes. Blond, curly-headed Merrill couldn't toddle very
far at eighteen months, but he often staggered the distance
to our sandpile to join the other neighborhood children. Pam
and Penny were the two Mead daughters. Pam had discovered the mobility of bicycles and usually played with
friends on another street. Penny, with her pert, freckled
nose and impish grin, had started first grade with Anne, and
the two were constant companions.

I had been leaning on my shovel, admiring Wanda's
flowers, and now realized with a start that it was time to go
indoors and make supper. The sun was as high in the sky as
midday, and it never got really dark at this time of year. A
kind of soft twilight would settle in about ten p.m., bright-
ening back to broad daylight by three in the morning. Next
week would come the longest day in the year, when Alaskans
celebrated by playing golf at midnight.

There was much about our adopted state, I thought as I started for the house, that I had yet to adjust to. We had been told that winters in the Anchorage area would be mild: "just like New England," Alaskans agreed. I shivered as I remembered the month-long spell of 30-degree-below-zero weather last Christmas. I'd hardly dared breathe out of doors, much less remain there longer than the dash for the car. Then we were lucky if the car started, and the tires felt square if we did get going. The short days were most unlike New England, too—the sun rising dimly through the ice fog around nine a.m. and disappearing abruptly around two-thirty in the afternoon.

The frosty air had a way, however, of turning anything it touched into glittering beauty—leaving a diamond-like coating over the snow cover that descended in mid-October and stayed until April each year. In fact, low places in our yard, like those curious parallel trenches near the bluff, still held patches of snow now in June. I loved this aspect of the Alaskan climate, compared to New England's rain and slush. The only drawback to the perpetual snow, I thought grimly, was clearing our driveway. Lowell had purchased a small plow to attach to our lumbering truck-like Travelall. But as he always seemed to be away when we had our big storms, it was I who had to hook up the thing and operate it—one of the many activities not covered by a liberal arts education.

Another was coping with the great, gawky wild moose who frequented our woods. Far larger than a horse, and the awkwardest-looking animal ever created, it was always a distinct surprise to encounter one while walking in the yard. "Don't worry," our Alaskan friends assured me (typically!), "the moose will run first." I believed that until early one morning when I opened the door to let Bozie outside. A gigantic mama moose was placidly chewing on my sweet-pea vines about five feet from our front steps, her calf just behind her. She immediately lowered her head and charged right at us. If I hadn't reacted instantly, she would have roared right on into the hall. Fortunately I managed to pull the dog back in with me and slam the door just in time. I shook for the rest of the day, while our mighty German Shepherd cowered on the couch.

Supper ready, I called Lowell from the study and the kids from the back yard. Like me they always had trouble believing it was "nighttime" with the sun high in the sky. I was clearing the plates away for dessert when all of us heard a distant roar. Another jet taking off from the nearby airport, I thought. But at the same time I felt an unexplainable dizziness, almost as though the house itself was moving. I glanced up at the hanging lamp above our heads. It was swaying briskly. As the walls around us began to creak, the children looked at us apprehensively.

Lowell, the calmest of the calm, smiled back at them. "Gee, kids, I think we're having a little earthquake—isn't it fun!" In the brief pause that followed, they were both obviously trying to decide just what was fun about it. I was trembling, palms sweaty, my heart pounding. Lowell shot me a "don't alarm the kids, but . . ." glance and continued just as calmly, "Why don't we go outside and watch the trees wave?"

There was a mild rush for the front door—the children now apparently just curious, but I feeling growing panic and claustrophobia in the small, swaying kitchen. We stood on the grass outdoors, watching those giant trees all around us sway back and forth, even the sturdiest ones which the wind merely ruffled. Anne cried, "Look at the car, Daddy, it's bouncing up and down!" Through the open door of the garage we all stared at the crazy gyrations of our station wagon. Then all at once everything grew still again. "A gentle tremor," Lowell concluded—no damage, nothing to worry about.

But I was terrified, and Lowell admitted, as we went to bed that night, that he had been "slightly concerned," too. "I really felt, for some reason or other, that it was safest for us to be out of doors," he mused. And then, characteristically, he dropped off to sleep while I lay awake for hours, shaken to the depths of my being by the "gentle tremor." So much of existence is uncertain, I thought wretchedly, and I've worked so hard to develop even a small sense of trust in it. But if the basis of everything, the most solid, most dependable thing we know, the very ground beneath our feet, is unstable and unpredictable too—then what certainty can there ever be?

I found myself thinking of those trenches in our yard. I simply had not been able to conceive of a force that could wrench the very earth apart. Now I could, and sweat poured from me as I faced the deep-down knowledge that absolutely nothing on this earth is fixed or sure.

In the weeks that followed this experience, I found myself back in my state of perpetual anxiety, of feeling alone and isolated, regardless of our new-found friends and our treasured home and belongings. Again I realized how desperately I needed some kind of basic foundation within me, some sort of stability which would enable me to face the changing and the unexpected—the kind of serenity I'd seen on the faces of the Eskimos at Point Hope.

In some of the people at St. Mary's—people like Chuck Harris—I'd glimpsed this same quality. And so I turned to them, to the church, with a greater urgency than I'd ever known before. Sandy Zabriskie's office had already become a familiar refuge in my battle with sleeping pills. Now Sandy provided me with books to read, and a gentle hint (which I acted on at once) that I start attending his Bible study class.

The other person I turned to at St. Mary's was Billie Williams, a kind of institution in herself. Billie devoted many hours a week to visiting native patients at the local Public Health Service Hospital. Most of these people had traveled so far from their villages to enter the hospital that they had few other callers. I tagged along once in a while, embarrassed by the natural reticence of the native people, finding real trouble in communicating with them. Not Billie. She breezed into the rooms, lugging a bunch of comic books and a well-worn guitar, laughing, teasing, asking about news from home. Faces lit up everywhere she went, and halls were often filled with laughter and singing in a most un-hospital-like way.

Billie was just as direct with her other volunteer work, shunning social fund-raising events and other arm's-length ways of helping others. She regularly assisted, for example, in classrooms for handicapped children—little ones so dreadfully disfigured and pathetic in behavior that many people, including myself, avoided personal contact. And though she herself was a busy wife and mother of three children she often gave up a night's sleep to sit with an alcoholic or someone else in emotional distress. (I was still battling the conviction that less than eight hours' sleep a night would leave me a tottering invalid.)

One day, when Billie's eyes were sparkling and she was as full of fun as usual, although I knew she had been up all night with a couple having marital problems, I bluntly asked her what her secret was, how she found so much energy and strength. She was quiet for a moment, rare for Billie, and then said, "I don't use it up in worry, I guess." She added, with her usual deep laugh, "God never runs out of power." I stared at her, not understanding. Billie never preached or talked "religion" with me; she simply lived her full life, including me in some of it.

I noticed other people at St. Mary's who, like Billie, like Chuck, radiated an inner serenity, who gave continuously of themselves with a cheerful willingness that was simply beyond my comprehension. If they saw a need they could fill, they were there, as I discovered the following fall when I had to undergo emergency surgery for a tubular preg-nancy. Whenever Lowell could not be at the hospital, these friends from St. Mary's were, talking, praying with me, simply sitting in the room. One morning Sandy brought the Holy Communion to me. Five parishioners came with him, forming a circle of caring around my bed, for a few moments turning that bleak hospital ward into a sanctuary.

Perhaps because the setting was so different from any communion service I'd ever attended, I found myself hearing the words as though for the very first time. I was stunned by what they said.

> . . . And here we offer and present unto thee, O Lord, ourselves, our souls and bodies . . .

Was this really what I'd repeated hundreds of times in the big stone church in Greenwich? When Sandy and the others had gone I lay staring at the ridge my feet made in the white hospital bed clothes. *We offer thee ourselves* . . .

Of course! This was Billie's secret, the secret of every real Christian. It wasn't a matter of giving God an hour every Sunday morning and some handmade items for the women's bazaar. God wanted all our time, every day. He wanted us, soul and body, nothing held back.

Being me, naturally, I could not take such a momentous step without much hesitation. For weeks after I left the hospital I agonized over it, trying to foresee all the consequences. Could I really hand over control of my life in one immense act of trust? Could I lay aside my fears and reservations and count on God to handle things? Would He take care of Lowell and the children, my own health and strength? Everything I was reading and observing, everything I was discovering in Sandy's class, assured me that He would—and do a far better job than I was doing.

Again, being me, I did not finally take this step in some embarrassing public way. I did it in my own car one February night driving home from a Bible class. It was eight months after the earth tremor that had started me searching in earnest for the source of true security. It was pitch dark —it was never much else this time of year—and I was all alone. As the windshield wipers slapped against a steady drizzle of sleet I said aloud,

"All right, Lord. I'm totally yours."

Even as I spoke, that station wagon seemed to fill with peace. It was the peace I experienced when holding my little plaque at bedtime, or reading the poem pasted to the dashboard of the airplane. But this was stronger, surer, full of knowledge of where the peace was coming from. I started to sing. I sang every hymn I could remember at the top of my lungs all the way home. It wasn't until I switched off the ignition in the garage that I realized I'd driven all the way without once slamming on the brakes in panic. Ordinarily I hated the icy roads and finished every winter errand with a churning stomach and a racing heart.

I noticed this unaccustomed calm many times in the months that followed. I discovered that it helped to repeat my act of self-surrender at the start of each day: "I put today in Your hands, Lord. I trust You to handle whatever comes up." At night too I (usually) remembered to thank Him for His support during the day, and to ask for forgiveness for my own failures.

The nightly list of errors and omissions, in fact, grew longer and longer as during the summer and fall of 1963 I took on every volunteer job I heard about. With work came responsibility. I was elected president of St. Mary's Churchwomen, president of the Women's Republican Club. I collapsed into bed every night exhausted, but—this was what Christianity was all about, wasn't it? Giving up yourself to serve others? Compared with many others I wasn't doing nearly enough, and I'd redouble my efforts.

In January 1964 I took on the chairmanship of the Easter Seal drive (raising money for Billie's handicapped children) and from then on I never got to bed before midnight. "You can make it till Easter and then it will be over," I kept telling myself.

But by the morning of Good Friday I was wondering if I actually could make it through the next two days. The reports on the various fund-raising events to go over, the final financial tally to draw up—certainly I was too tired to get to St. Mary's for the Good Friday service. Too tired to do anything but pick up the house and try to remember where I'd put the children's Easter baskets . . .

7.

Speak Through the Earthquake

It was snowing, too, and in late March, after five solid months of it, I was heartily sick of winter. I was worried as well, as I looked out our living room window toward Turnagain Arm. The visibility was so poor I could barely see the other shore, and the gray clouds seemed to hang just above our trees. Lowell had gone to the airport after lunch, planning to fly to Fairbanks and, as usual, I felt great apprehension over his going in such weather. I knew he had to go—much that he was discovering about our adopted state, especially the conditions under which the native people lived, aroused his concern, and he had decided to try for his first political office.

Getting involved in politics would mean a lot of flying for Lowell during the coming summer and fall, and many hours of anxiety on my part. No matter how much progress I was making learning to trust God in certain areas of our lives, I'd never been able to relax as long as Lowell was up in that little plane. I felt so tired that I longed to lie down and just sleep for a week.

I heard the sound of an airliner overhead, and as I stared through the gloom to look for it, remembered that I was supposed to be at the airport at that very moment. The Women's Republican Club was putting on a farewell celebration there for one of our members who had won the Mrs. Alaska contest and was leaving Anchorage at five-thirty for the national pageant.

They'd just have to manage without me; I couldn't face another official duty. How did people like Billie do it, I wondered for the thousandth time—accomplish the work of six with never a sign of weariness? The snow had begun to let up, turning to rain as so often happened in late March. The visibility was better, too: I could see the cliffs and trees on the opposite shoreline. One good thing about March, there were many more hours of light each day. Lowell and the weather forecaster were right, I thought a little grudgingly. The weather outlook had been for improvement by mid-afternoon, and on the strength of that report, Lowell had left for the airport four hours earlier. He'd have taken off by now . . .

Eight-year-old Anne, and Dave, now six, had been playing together at the far end of the living room with Dave's collection of miniature cars and a felt cloth on which I'd appliqued city streets. Now Anne came to me, putting her head on my lap. "Mother, I have an awful headache."

I stroked her hair for a while, then suggested we go up and lie on her bed together for a little rest before supper.

She readily agreed, obviously in pain, and Dave allowed that he'd come along and watch the TV set in Lowell's and my bedroom, just across the hall. He and Anne were dressed in their usual blue jeans and cotton shirts, and both dutifully took off their shoes as Dave flopped onto our bed, and Anne curled up beside me on hers. It was a joy to slip out of my own shoes—I felt as if I'd been on my feet all week. I was still wearing a red wool dress and stockings—formal attire for me around the house, but I'd had an Easter Seal campaign meeting earlier.

It was about 5:35 p.m. then, and as I lay on Anne's bed, rubbing her forehead to help the ache, I heard a distant rumble. It wasn't an airplane. Anne's window faced nearby Fort Richardson and we often heard the reverberation of the guns. I knew instantly, however, that this was not guns, either. This was the sound of an earthquake.

Like a performer who'd been rehearsing for this moment all my life, perhaps reacting subconsciously to Lowell's example nearly two years before, I leapt off the bed, pulling Anne by the hand. As we raced for the bedroom door I called to Dave: "Come on, let's go outside, it's another little earthquake!" He was beside us in an instant. By the time we had run down the four steps into the front hall, the whole house was beginning to shake.

As I opened the front door, Dave yelled, "But Mommy, I'm in my bare feet!" I grabbed his hand, pulling him out. "That's okay, we'll just stay out a moment." Anne was right beside me; she had not said a word. We had reached the snow-covered lawn about ten feet from the front steps when we were all flung violently to the ground. The earth was jolting back and forth with unbelievable force, the world around us literally falling apart.

As I lay, half stunned, on the snow, the children whimpering beside me, I watched the hallway through which we had just run split in two. We heard the crashing of glass, the ear-rending sound of splintering wood. I stared in disbelief as the whole front wall fell inward, revealing the kitchen. I caught a glimpse of the new yellow refrigerator and stove, then sections of the roof began collapsing, burying them beneath a jumbled mass of beams and shingles.

I heard a loud crash behind us, and turned to see one of our giant pine trees thunder to the ground. The trees were all whipping back and forth wildly, many looked as if they were about to fall. I recalled how they had only swayed gently during that earlier quake, then remembered how the car had bounced in the garage. I looked in that direction just in time to see the garage walls and roof collapse on the station wagon.

The ground had been shaking violently all the while. Suddenly I heard a sharp cracking noise beside me and watched in horror as dirt began to show beneath the deep layer of snow—dark brown against the stark white. The earth was beginning to break up all about us, and a large fissure was opening between Anne and me. I stared in disbelief as the trench widened, apparently bottomless, separating me from my child. I quickly seized the hand she stretched out to me and pulled her across the chasm to my side.

By now the whole lawn was breaking up into bigger and smaller chunks of frozen, snow-covered dirt. The three of us were marooned on a wildly bucking little slab; suddenly it tilted sharply and we began to slip backward into the yawning crevasse at our feet. I grabbed hold of the jagged edge with one hand, and clung tightly to Dave with the other. He was hysterical now, crying over and over. "We're going to die!" Though crying, too, Anne had the presence of mind to hang on by herself.

Grappling for a firmer hold in this chaos, clinging to my little boy, I thought suddenly: we're seeing the end of the world! The Bible class recently had focused on this subject, and following the first thought came another: if the world is ending, Jesus is coming! As our slab of dirt and snow tipped even more steeply, I looked eagerly up into the low gray clouds. I wasn't sure whether I would see Him descending in a white robe surrounded by a shining light, or seated at the side of God on a great throne supported by angels. But I was absolutely confident that I would see Him.

I stared at the wisps of gray mist trailing downward from the solid overcast, wondering if the cloud curtain would simply part to reveal Him, or if the whole sky would vanish as the earth was doing. Neither thing happened. And yet at that moment I was aware of the most intense, indescribable peace I had ever felt.

It was more than peace; it was the certain, unmistakable knowledge of His presence. Not way up in the sky above us. Beside us, around us, in us—His closeness bringing an assurance and support such as I had never experienced before. It was as though He was telling me that I was not alone and in the midst of utter catastrophe had nothing at all to be worried about.

Our chunk of earth was moving backwards now, backwards and down, like a monstrous ferris wheel traveling in reverse. In the calm of His extraordinary presence I looked around me almost with detachment. There was the children's bright yellow swing set, jauntily sitting on a chunk of ground all its own, floating by us as in a crazy dream. My little greenhouse passed us, too. Still in one piece, not a pane of glass broken. That's odd, I thought, because the swing had been in the back yard, close to the edge of the cliff, while the greenhouse had been in front of the house, next to the driveway. Now they had completely shifted positions in a world without rules.

Suddenly the massive earth slide came to an end, our little slab jerking to a stop in a jumbled mass of snow, dirt and blue clay. Bits and pieces of our house and garage were lying all about us, the red paint of the walls standing out starkly against the snow and dirt of the tumbled ground. Looking around I saw that the entire face of the bluff had fallen to sea level. A few feet away, at the water's edge, lay the roof of our house. Water . . . suddenly I recalled the stories I'd heard of tidal waves following after earthquakes.

We must get away from the water! But the new cliff face above us was perpendicular, with great sections of sand and clay still falling. It appeared to be an impassable barrier, steep and hazardous. For the first time I noticed the Bashaw home, once across the street from us, but now perched on the very edge of the precipice. Their front yard had vanished; instead, just beyond their front door a large broken pipe protruded from the cliff, water pouring from its gaping mouth.

I scanned the rest of the cliff on both sides of the Bashaw home, and could see no break in that sheer high barrier. Obviously we'd have to walk parallel to it to try to find a way out, but how would we pick our way among the crazily tilted slabs of earth? Everywhere trees leaned at perilous angles and lengths of electrical wires sparked and snapped.

Anne and Dave were both hysterical now, clinging to me, saying over and over, "We'll die, we'll die!" I realized that they were too frightened to walk and obviously I would not be able to carry both of them. I put my arms around them and begged them to quiet down.

Then I heard myself suggesting that we kneel for a moment and say a prayer, asking Jesus to take care of us. I had never prayed this way with the children before, only the brief, formal Now-I-lay-me-down-to-sleep kind at bedtime, but the suggestion did not feel strange to me, and they accepted the idea just as matter-of-factly. Both stopped crying, dropped to their knees and closed their eyes: "Please, Jesus, take care of us, don't let us die!" The prayer took just a moment, but it had an immediate calming effect on both of them.

Now for the first time I heard other voices. It sounded like children crying, and I turned anxiously toward where the Mead house had stood. Their roof lay at the edge of the water, small bits and pieces of what had been their dream house were scattered over the snow. Then I saw two small forms clinging to the roof of their car, which was also at the foot of the cliff. I started struggling over the broken ground toward them, but every route I tried was blocked. Anne and Dave fell flat a dozen times and I finally realized we could make no progress in that direction. I shouted to the Mead children to remain on their firm perch for the moment and I'd go for help.

We started off the other way. The next ten minutes were one great nightmare as we clambered up and down great slabs of slippery blue clay and snow, our bare feet aching and raw in the cold. I had to carry Dave part of the way, and lift Anne over obstacles. We found a large tree leaning against the cliff and thought for a few moments that we might be able to shinny up it, but we gained only a few feet. We kept moving to the right, trying to avoid the holes which opened at our feet and rubble still falling from the cliff.

Suddenly a man appeared above us. "Help!" all three of us called at once. He shouted down that he would hunt for a rope, then disappeared. As we waited we became aware for the first time that we were soaked to the skin from lying in the snow; the children were shaking and their lips were blue. I kept glancing back at the sea: had the water risen since I looked last? Our dog Bozie, too, and the cat, and the one kitten we had kept—what had happened to them? Had they been trapped in the house, or had they made it out over the collapsing walls?

At last a group of six or eight men appeared at the top of the cliff. One of them, a young fellow in his early twenties, started down the embankment a little way off. I could see now that there was a possible route up at that point—the slope was more gradual, with a mound of dirt just beneath the rim that we might be able to use as a final handhold.

The children both rushed toward our rescuer, hugging him tightly, talking about how cold they were. He took off his black wool jacket and put it around Anne. After getting her assurance that she could climb on her own, he swept Dave up into his arms and started up.

I followed, the dirt and sand slipping beneath my feet,

wondering how the young man could be so surefooted. He was almost at the rim now, with Anne crawling along right behind him. I got down on my hands and knees, too, ripping my dress—my stockings were already in shreds. When I reached the sheer section just beneath the lip, I was sure I could not scale it, but willing hands reached down to haul me up. I thought, "Why, I don't have to do anything. They're doing it for me." It was as though a heavy load of responsibility was being lifted from me as well.

At the top of the cliff I turned to thank the children's rescuer, but he had disappeared, the only tangible evidence of his presence the black wool jacket draped around Anne's shoulders. I was telling the other men about the two Mead children when I caught sight of Wanda Mead, standing with a little group of onlookers, her face strained and white. I fervently hoped my report would be good news, but I was all too aware that there were three other Mead children still to be accounted for.

There was no chance to talk to her as Anne, Dave and I were hurried to a pickup truck, and before I could get a good look at what had happened to our lovely street, we were whisked away. The driver said he was taking us to his home a few blocks away. We stopped in front of a house which looked completely intact, except for the front steps which were a pile of rubble. He and his wife rushed us inside, gave us armfuls of blankets, and invited us to stretch out on two large couches.

Without heat or electricity the house was cold, and I told the children to take off their wet clothes, wrap themselves in the blankets, and rub their feet gently. I slipped out of my soaked and torn wool dress, and did the same. The children became cheerful, even gleeful, as we coaxed feeling back into our feet. The resilience of little ones, I thought, and was beginning to relax a bit myself when the house was shaken by a violent tremor.

At the sound of the creaking wood and rattling windows I jumped from the couch in terror. Screaming hysterically, the children and I, still wrapped in our blankets, rushed headlong out of doors.

Our somewhat bewildered hosts tried to calm us down and persuade us to come back inside. But I wasn't about to go back beneath a roof, and the children vehemently agreed, although we were all three shivering with cold. When it became obvious that we weren't going to budge, the man suggested that we sit in his pickup truck, parked in the street.

We huddled there for about thirty minutes, feeling the earth constantly tremble beneath us, watching the trees wave back and forth. Men and women from the undamaged houses around us were standing in small groups along the street, and I was surprised to sense no panic among them. There were few signs of earthquake damage here, however; perhaps many of them were still unaware of the catastrophic results of the quake along the bluff line.

I decided to try the truck radio, and was overwhelmed to discover that one of Anchorage's four stations was still on the air, using emergency power. The announcer was saying matter-of-factly that the present tremors were only normal aftershocks, no cause for alarm. He kept repeating, "Stay in your homes or cars and wait for further word." He added that as far as was known at that point the quake had caused little damage. "Wait till he sees our street!" Anne snorted indignantly.

People were beginning to bring armloads of blankets and food from their homes, loading up their cars. It looked as if they had decided to move their families further away from the bluff area. This was fine with me—I tried to keep in check an intense urgency to move on instantly, especially when the announcer began broadcasting a possible tidal wave alert.

Where should we go? At other times I would have turned to my Chilligan neighbors for help. It was getting dark and for the first time since the start of the quake, I felt very alone. Then I thought of St. Mary's and the Zabriskies next door in the rectory. That's where we'd go! Perhaps we could even stay in the church basement a few days if necessary.

Now that I was starting to think about the future, I realized for the first time that we had nothing left in the way of possessions except the clothes we had escaped in. I thought of my treasured antiques, my cherished silver, but even as they came to mind I knew they were unimportant. How could I ever have connected them with permanence? I remembered the walls and roof caving in like a deck of cards, crushing everything beneath. I almost laughed out loud as I recalled counting on my precious belongings for security. Now, in the very moment of realizing that everything was gone, I knew that what really mattered was people —how thankful I felt that we had escaped alive! People . . . and more than that: a Person whom I had known, however briefly, to be Security itself.

The aftershocks were continuing and I was greatly relieved when the couple who had taken us in were ready to leave. The wife drove their car, filled with children and belongings, while her husband led the way with the pickup truck and the three of us. He had just made another trip to Chilligan Drive and reported that everyone now seemed to be accounted for except two of the Mead children. My heart rose in my throat—could they be the two I'd seen standing on the car?

As we drove through the eerily-dark streets of Turnagain I was appalled at the deep cracks in the paved roads—gaping, jagged fissures which looked bottomless. When would we come to one that was too wide to cross? Eventually, however, we reached the main highway. I had had nightmare visions of roads jammed with panicky motorists fleeing from the shoreline, but most of the cars were emergency vehicles with flashing lights, and I noticed National Guardsmen directing traffic at the dark intersections. The whole area was in inky blackness with no electricity, pierced only by the blinking warning lights and clanging bells along some abandoned railroad tracks. The mechanical system must have been triggered by the shaking earth; they would probably blink and clang away needlessly throughout the night.

A few more moments, and we were climbing the hill toward the church and rectory. Both buildings were dark, and I worried for a moment that no one was there. What would we do then? The rectory, home to the Zabriskies, seemed to be undamaged, and I rushed up the pathway. I felt greatly comforted when Sandy opened the front door, and put his arms around all three of us.

We bid a thankful goodbye to our first benefactor, but almost immediately realized that we were faced with another temporary situation. The house was cold, dark and a mess inside. There had been little structural damage, but the kitchen cabinets had been flung open, depositing food over counter tops and floor. The living room carpet was also liberally sprinkled with broken glass, books and toys—whatever had been on the shelves. Sandy's wife Margie and their four children had just left to spend the night elsewhere.

Sandy took over for the moment, and for this leadership I was deeply grateful. First he found some candles, then he brought us a platter of cold roast beef and a carving knife. The children reacted in childlike fashion—they forgot their fears and remembered that they were hungry (it was now about eight-thirty). The candles meant a party, and it didn't matter that the meat was almost raw. Doubtless the quake had knocked out the oven before the roast was finished cooking. No forks, plates or napkins were needed, either, as I whacked off big chunks of cold meat which the kids gobbled up. Their spirit was so contagious that I even ate a little myself.

While we were eating, Sandy collected some clothing for the kids, a difficult undertaking in the pitch-dark house, made harder because all his children were younger than Anne and Dave. We began to laugh over some of the items the children put on—over-sized boots of Margie's for Anne (to match her man-sized jacket), pants for Dave which came only to his hips, needing several safety pins to close them safely. I was having the same problem as I rummaged through Margie's drawers in the darkness. She was considerably smaller than I, and I finally gave up and helped myself to a pair of Sandy's corduroy work pants and a wool shirt.

Just when warmth was returning to our bodies and spirits, another strong tremor shook the house. All calm deserted me, and I rushed for the door—the children were well ahead of me. I did stop long enough to blow out the candles. Then, as I ran in the darkness toward the door, I fell over the Zabriskies' large brown dog. I landed with a crash, and the two bruises I sustained from this silly encounter were the first injuries any of us had so far suffered.

By the time I had picked myself up, the tremor was over and Sandy was assuring us that we needn't worry about the aftershocks. I wanted to believe him, but the instinctive desire to run was too strong, and throughout that long night of terror, when the area was almost constantly hit by tremors, the children and I rushed for the door every time. How ironic, I thought, that I had been able to cope so efficiently with the real emergency, and now fell apart with every little quiver.

Sandy's Senior Warden came by the house at that point to see if all was under control. He and his wife lived in a spacious home high on the hillside and had suffered almost no damage except loss of electricity. Obviously it made sense for us to go there for the night, although I did not know them and was reluctant to leave Sandy's comforting guidance.

So off we went again. It had begun to snow heavily again, and the road was a sheet of ice. My thoughts, since we were assured of shelter for the night, were all about Lowell now. Surely he had heard about the devastating earthquake, and must be worrying terribly, perhaps even trying to return in this bad weather. How could I get word to him that we were safe? I wondered if the tremor had affected Fairbanks, but doubted it because that interior city lay far from the Pacific Rim seismic zone.

Our new quarters looked normal in every way, except for kerosene lantern light, and there were two spare bedrooms at our disposal. When I tried to put the children to bed, however, they flatly refused, and insisted, instead, on remaining beside me in the living room. I understood how they felt—I had already made up my own mind that I'd stay on the couch nearest to the front door! So our hostess put sleeping bags for them on the living room floor. They were soon asleep, but both awoke whenever there was a tremor, crying in terror, running with me to the door.

I curled up under several blankets, but sleep was out of the question. I was increasingly concerned about getting in touch with Lowell. All telephone lines were down, so there was no way to get a message out. The best thing, I decided, was to monitor the radio constantly, and I placed a small transistor set on the arm of the couch.

I listened for hours, hearing for the first time of the terrible devastation that had occurred in other parts of Anchorage. Experts were reporting that the quake had registered 8.4 on the Richter scale, the strongest ever recorded on the North American continent. The city had called in the National Guard (fortuitously they were on maneuvers in the Anchorage area this month) and the local police organized teams of volunteers from the mountain rescue group to help search the hard-hit sections for casualties.

I learned that all the homes on the bluff in Turnagain-by-the-Sea had been destroyed by the slide, about one hundred in all. A large section of downtown Fourth Avenue had simply sunk, dropping sidewalks and buildings as much as thirty feet. The recently opened five-story J. C. Penney store, pride of the community, had crumbled onto the street, and a new eight-story apartment house in the west end of town, mercifully still unoccupied, had collapsed.

All night long over the radio came plaintive requests to locate loved ones. "The Abbott family want to know the whereabouts of daughter Jean," or: "Tell John his parents are at the Stewarts'," and: "Does anyone know where Anne Read and her children have gone?" Not only had many young people taken off skiing because of the Easter holiday, but mothers and fathers had not yet returned from work. I felt that family separation would be particularly difficult and was grateful over and over that I had not gone to the party at the airport.

Sandwiched between the personal appeals were terse disaster headquarters communiques and urgent requests for personnel and supplies from the two local hospitals. I winced each time I heard, "Will Dr. Mead please report to Providence Hospital emergency room?" I heard later that Dr. Mead answered these pleas for help with tears streaming down his face—two of his own children were still missing.

The shock of the continuous reports of destruction was alleviated somewhat by the reassuring news of low loss of life. As the night wore on, it became apparent that despite the terrible damage, only eight people had been killed in the Anchorage area. Of these, two were Mead children, but the radio did not give their names. I thought of mature, responsible young Perry, pretty Pam, Anne's friend Penny with her impish grin, will-of-the-wisp Paul, cuddly, adorable little Merrill—no, it just couldn't be any of them!

About three a.m. the radio announcer told of a Wien Airlines project flying to Anchorage from Fairbanks, bringing doctors and supplies. I knew then that Lowell would be on board that plane; the airline's head pilot, undoubtedly flying that night, was Merrill Wien, one of Lowell's close friends. Lowell and I had both flown with Merrill under many tough conditions—if he was at the controls no snowstorm would stop them.

Sure enough, an hour later the broadcaster said, "If anyone knows the whereabouts of Mrs. Lowell Thomas Jr. and family, please contact us immediately." I ran to the phone to try again to call the station, and was so stunned to discover it working that I could hardly talk to the person who answered. I got the essential information over, however, and within a half hour, in the first light of dawn, I saw our Travelall truck come bouncing along the rutted street.

I practically laughed out loud at the sight of that large, awkward, muddy vehicle—I thought it had disappeared along with the house! I had forgotten that Lowell had driven it to the airport; now it was like receiving a Christmas present to realize we had one material possession left.

Words cannot describe our reunion with Lowell—of course the children and I were tremendously relieved to have him with us again, but Lowell's feelings were those of a man who had not known whether his family were dead or alive for many hours. The earthquake had hit just before he landed at Fairbanks, barely setting the ground in motion there. Lowell heard almost immediately, however, that Anchorage, and particularly the Turnagain area, had been hard hit. In fact, first reports seeping out via ham radio told of our end of town being completely destroyed.

Hitching the first available ride back to Anchorage, he found the entire Turnagain area roped off, with no one allowed to enter. At disaster headquarters, officials asked where he lived; when he mentioned Chilligan Drive, there was a strained silence. Finally one young man gently suggested that he send a message out over the radio.

All I wanted to do, now that we were reunited, was to cling to him and talk, but he felt he should apply for a permit to enter the area immediately, to look for the dog and cats, and to see if he could salvage any of our belongings. I dreaded ever going back there again, and hated to see him leave, but I kept busy in the meantime with the practical problems of cooking breakfast over a campstove. I also had my hands full with two hyperactive children—their laughter and shouts convinced me they would quickly return to normal!

They were particularly happy when they saw their father returning with Bozie trotting beside him, and Dave's black kitten, Sylvester, in his arms. (Mama cat was found beneath a pile of clothing the following day, unscathed, but doubtless having used up eight of her nine lives.) Lowell had found the dog howling mournfully beside the remains of the house, the kitten nearby.

It wasn't long before we began to locate our scattered neighbors and to hear the stories of their harrowing experiences. The relief of seeing someone again, alive and well, was unbelievable. For weeks, all over Anchorage, people would dash across a street to throw their arms around newly recovered friends. Humor made a speedy comeback; Turnagain-by-the-Sea was inevitably renamed Turnagain-in-the Sea.

But as we rejoiced with one another over our escapes, we were acutely conscious of the tragedy suffered by the Meads. Lowell and I could not learn for several days which two children had been lost, or how it happened. Wanda had gone to the store on an errand, and Pam, the oldest girl, was visiting friends. The story had to come from Anne's playmate, Penny, and her little brother, Paul, who had climbed to the roof of their car parked in the driveway. (They were the two I had seen.) Young Perry, who had been left in charge, had helped them from the collapsing house, then returned to save baby Merrill. No trace of Perry or the baby was ever found.

In the days and weeks that followed, we dug out many of our belongings from the wreckage of the house. Our precious photo albums and movie reels emerged undamaged, but the furniture was largely destroyed. We found a few pieces badly broken but still fixable. Other items of furniture had simply vanished, perhaps into some bottomless crevasse. The Sheraton sideboard and the blue silk couch were never seen again, but the dainty Hepplewhite table, with its glass top, came through unscathed. So did one of our favorite wedding presents, a dainty crystal vase. Lowell found it sitting on top of a mound of clay, as if on display in a store window.

I was deeply thankful for each item we recovered, but

also aware that my attitude toward our belongings had completely changed. I had no feeling of dependency on them anymore; they were no longer my "security blanket." Even when I discovered my much-loved prayer plaque in the rubble, I knew it would never have the same meaning for me. As a symbol it had served its function; during the quake I had tasted the reality behind all symbolism.

Easter Sunday, 1964, will always have a special place in my memories—and it won't be a vision of floral hats and egg hunts for the children. The church was cold, still without heat or electricity, and we and many of our homeless friends clumped down the aisle in borrowed clothing. Anne was still wearing her rescuer's jacket, far more meaningful to her than a new Easter bonnet. (We were never able to locate or even identify that young man.) Dave was patiently holding up his pants, and I was still clad in Sandy's corduroy pants and wool shirt. As far as we knew then, those were the only clothes we owned.

The singing, with no electricity to run the organ, had never sounded so beautiful, and the spiritual warmth had never been so noticeable. Prayers of thanksgiving took on an intense depth of meaning, especially the Epistle for Easter Day:

> If ye then be risen with Christ, seek those things which are above, where Christ sitteth on the right hand of God. Set your affection on things above, not on things on the earth . . .
>
> Colossians 3:1, 2, KJV

"Things on earth". . . I had seen them disappear into bottomless holes, and for one brief instant I had had an experience of "things above." It was an unseen world which remained unseen. But Christ had been there, more real, more tangible and comforting than all the physical things which had disappeared around me.

Before the service ended, Sandy announced that two lists had been placed in the entryway, one for the "haves," those families who had clothing and household goods they might wish to contribute, and a second sheet where those who had lost everything could write down what they needed. That morning at least 20 of St. Mary's 125 families were homeless, and yet, by the end of the three Sunday services, the "have" list was over four pages long, while only two names stood on the "have not" sheet, both placed there by Sandy himself!

For just what was there we did not have? We only felt a deep thankfulness for the gift of life, for having survived one of history's worst earthquakes. Now the exciting challenge of rebuilding our state lay ahead of us, as each of us felt a new love for our Alaska and its citizens who had shown such courage and concern for one another. And we shared the Easter message with new conviction: the dreams and hopes of the first Christians had collapsed in ruins too on that sorrowful first Good Friday. Then on Sunday morning they began to spread the news that has transformed every loss from that day on—the news that God had the final word, that death had been overcome, that He had risen.

And I had one further message on which to ponder long and hard. Something had happened to me that day, when it seemed like the world was coming to an end. For a few brief moments I had risen above my fears and anxieties—for a little while I had known the living presence of Jesus Christ, and felt His peace which was beyond human understanding. Whatever happened in the months and years ahead, I knew that my first and most important goal had to be to find Him again.

8.

Wind Through the Pine Trees

Throughout the summer and winter following the earthquake much of my time was devoted to resettling—first in a temporary house, part of a new subdivision. Our furniture was sparse, each piece a much appreciated donation from the basements of friends. Then we bought some wooded land several miles inland from the bluff (I carefully checked geologists' reports first!) and launched into our first venture of building a home. Four other former Chilligan Drive neighbors had chosen the same place, another quiet dirt road, and while we could never recreate the Turnagain setting, we hoped to develop one similar in character.

I also plunged back into community activities. Much of that first year had to be spent simply reestablishing records: every box, file and book for the Churchwomen, the Republican Club and the Easter Seal campaign had been swallowed up by the earth. As the pace of life speeded up again I continued to set aside time each day for the search that was my first priority. I spent more time than ever reading the Bible and other inspirational books and taking part in church study groups. But my life was too cluttered with distractions and busyness for real concentration. And it was then that I discovered the church's Birchwood retreat camp in the wilderness north of Anchorage. At Birchwood I could leave the clutter behind and be part of a group of seeking Christians.

During my first retreat, I took a rowboat out alone onto the small lake around four o'clock one morning. The air was cool and damp, and patches of mist clung to the dark surface of the water. The Alaskan summer day was already bright, but the towering mountain peaks which rimmed the valley still shielded the lake from the direct rays of the sun.

The air was as still and quiet as the water—I was one very small human being in the silent vastness of the Alaskan wilderness. The oar locks squeaked slightly so I stopped rowing for a while, drifting almost imperceptibly toward shore. "Be still and know that I am God." I could almost hear the command echo down through ages. O God, how I would like just to sit here until I unraveled Your mysteries!

The silence was absolute for many long moments, and then I heard the melancholy call of a loon. I stared through the mist and was startled to discover I wasn't really alone. Two loons were treading water lazily about fifty feet away, staring incuriously back. They finally made the first move, suddenly bobbing beneath the water in search of breakfast. I was sorry to lose their company; they had provided a companionship that enhanced rather than destroyed solitude.

As I drifted closer to the wooded shoreline I found another early riser. All I could see at first was a sleek brown head, but as he swam closer, the beaver's big, bright eyes looked right at me. I sensed in that brief moment of communication that he, too, knew why I was there. But he had his morning work ahead of him, and with his broad paddle tail propelling him, he headed back to shore.

I drifted in among the fallen logs and high cranberry bushes along the banks. I could hear birds now, but no sounds from the camp among the tall spruce trees. My human companions were asleep, snug in their sleeping bags on the bunks lining the walls of the little cabins, and the larger log building where we gathered to eat and work was empty and still—no smoke coming yet from the large stone chimney.

I pulled on one oar a few times to avoid a half-sunken log, and remembered the fun we had had swimming the day before. We had found a shallow area heated by the afternoon sun. One can swim so seldom out of doors in Alaska and I missed it terribly.

It had been glorious to sit on the float and talk and laugh with the young people who had come to the retreat from Indian villages in the far north. They'd wanted me to teach them to dive off the float. Following my instructions, three girls stood up and leaned toward the water, heads down between their outstretched arms. There, courage failed.

"I'm scared," one of them giggled nervously. "Are you sure I'll come back up?" "Of course," I laughed, "just trust me. You'll pop right back up like corks." At last they seemed convinced, and all three splashed in. They surfaced immediately, beaming from ear to ear. And of course they had to repeat it over and over, laughing constantly at themselves and each other.

As I sat on the float watching, I'd thought about my own plunge into the Christian walk. The act of commitment that night in the car over two years before had been a lot like diving headfirst into an unfamiliar element, just as these girls had done. But something was wrong. My action somehow remained incomplete. It was true I'd experienced a period of peace and joy following the decision—and often since. But there'd also been times when fear and worry had proved stronger still. Much of the work I'd taken on in the first flush of love and gratitude to God had by now become mere drudgery. And when I was being truthful with myself I knew there were areas of fear and insecurity deep inside me which had never been healed.

As the bow of the boat swung around the old log, I could see the small natural amphitheater where we held our worship services, a horseshoe-shaped hollow in the high bank with rough built-in benches. Jesus would have loved the spot, I thought; I could almost picture Him there with His disciples around Him, sharing bread and fish.

We had gathered there the evening before to celebrate Communion. The centuries-old words of the opening prayer which I had memorized as a child had spoken to me in this setting in a new way. Like the mist rising now from the water around me, a veil had seemed to lift, revealing a previously unglimpsed landscape:

Almighty God, unto whom all hearts are open . . . cleanse the thoughts of our hearts by the inspiration of thy Holy Spirit . . .

The thoughts of my heart, I knew, were too often ones of anxiety and worry. Could the Holy Spirit really clean such things as this out of the mind and the personality? Maybe, I thought, when I gave my life to God that night in the car, it was my conscious mind I was turning over—those parts of my being over which I had control. But what about the other parts, those things I myself wasn't even aware of? Could the Holy Spirit deal with things like that? Who was the Holy Spirit, anyway, and how did He enter our lives?

The silence of the woods was suddenly shattered by loud

banging on cabin doors and shouts to "rise and shine." I rowed slowly back, reluctant to disturb the stillness of the water.

Back in Anchorage the following week I plunged into an effort to learn all I could about the Holy Spirit. I haunted the book stores, grabbing any volume that had the word *Spirit* on the cover. My collection became almost as large as my shelf of cookbooks. Some of my new purchases I discarded half-read, others I went over a number of times, underlining passages like a textbook.

In many of the books the word *charismatic* popped up again and again. I wasn't sure of the exact meaning of the word, except that the *charismatic movement* currently sweeping the country was concerned with the power and gifts of the Holy Spirit. When I learned that a local church was sponsoring a "charismatic clinic" I eagerly showed up for the first session.

As I stepped up to the registration table I was conscious of curious stares following me. It seemed to me that the entire vestibule was listening as I whispered to the registrar, "Could I sign up for the clinic?" "That will be $15.00," she said crisply, and I promptly lost the courage to ask if I could pay for just one day. I'd meant to explain that I was there on a trial basis, but somehow felt I would immediately be labeled a non-believer.

I slipped on into the large church and found a seat in one of the rear pews directly behind two bald-headed men. I was debating whether to take off my coat when a booming "Praise the Lord!" reverberated throughout the church. I almost jumped out of my skin, as well as the coat. The entire congregation replied in kind. This was repeated several times. At last I ventured a timid "Praise the Lord" of my own, whereupon both bald gentlemen turned and stared at me.

I might have stood up and fled at that point, but I was saved by the appearance of a singing group whose spirited music gave me a few moments to regain my composure. The minister then introduced a visiting "evangelist." I perked up because one of his books was among my growing collection at home. His first words were, "Raise your arms high and praise the Lord!" I had inched my hands up as far as my shoulders when my two gentlemen friends in front turned to check my performance. Some women across the aisle were eyeing me too and I began to feel like a spy in enemy territory.

The evangelist had been talking at least an hour and a half when suddenly a woman in one of the front pews jumped up and began shouting totally incomprehensible syllables. I was baffled—not only by the meaningless sounds she was making, but also by her audacity in interrupting the speaker. Even more surprising, every one around me seemed to accept her behavior as normal, even murmuring "amen" from time to time. This went on for several minutes and then the woman sat down, at least having effectively brought the evangelist to a halt, and the session to a close. I struggled into my coat and rushed for the exit, the first person to get out the door. Goodbye $15.00, I thought: if that is what *charismatic* means, they can have it.

I had felt far closer to the Holy Spirit in the early-morning solitude at Birchwood, and I began to look for chances to slip off alone into the out-of-doors. This was easier to say than to do in our hectic lives just then. Lowell had been elected to the state senate, which meant his commuting much of the winter to Juneau, the state capital. I was on the school board in Anchorage, and the children had reached the busy pre-teen years with a different activity after school every day. We could have kept four cars (with chauffeurs) and three telephones in constant use.

But whenever I could I fled into the woods behind our house, walking or skiing for an all-too-brief interlude. We had carved paths out of the thick undergrowth of our twenty acres, and it was spiritually refreshing just to wander about this beautiful miniature wilderness. The trees, unlike the giants around our Chilligan home, were secondary growth

—stands of tall, slim aspen and birch and waist-high evergreens. There was something special about the woods in deep winter, when snow blanketed the ground to a depth of several feet and etched each branch in sparkling white. At such times I could easily recapture that stillness I had found at Birchwood.

When the snow came, I put on my cross-country skis: the feeling of effortless gliding over the white surface recalled my little rowboat on the lake. Only I was a much better rower than a skier! I had many disastrous encounters with bumps on the trail, usually ending in an ignominious heap in the deep icy snow. If my skis began moving too fast, I grabbed at the trees to slow myself down. This maneuver inevitably ended with a load of snow from the upper branches falling down my neck.

In spite of my awkwardness, these were always joyful times. As on the lake, here too I wasn't really alone. Squirrels talked to me from the branches overhead. I often brought them peanuts, and was furiously scolded when I forgot. The white rabbits were more elusive, blending in so perfectly with the snowy landscape that I saw them only when I was close enough to look into their sharp black eyes. My only other companions I could just as soon have done without—the great, gawky brown moose. Usually I saw only their mammoth footprints in the deep snow. But every once in a while we met face to face, and it's hard to say which one of us retreated quickest; it was amazing how fast and easily I could ski then.

There, in the midst of my little private wilderness, I usually prayed aloud, sharing my thoughts, questions, joys and troubles with the Lord. At first I used the formal language of the prayer book, but as the weeks and months went by I began to feel more at ease. "Lord, I just can't handle that problem, can I dump it on you?" was my new vernacular. Other times there just weren't any words to express what I felt. Like the moment I caught a glimpse of the setting sun through the frosted branches of the trees, shafts of brilliant gold soaring up among pale pink clouds. I was bursting to share my joy with God but my vocabulary was inadequate. There was so much bubbling of emotion within me that words just seemed to get in the way.

Or the time when I knew I faced a second "repair" operation. My apprehension had built up to the point where I could only give a cry of despair. I stopped short on the snowy trail: hadn't I read somewhere in the Bible that God hears and understands the sighing of the Spirit? Was this another way to communicate with God? Perhaps this was what was meant by "speaking in tongues." The only time I had heard "ecstatic utterance"—that hysterical woman in the church that day—it had seemed to me ugly and embarrassing. But what if it were actually the Spirit within a human being speaking directly to God in a way the mind could not comprehend?

Back to my books for another eager search which at last provided the key to my quest for the Spirit. I didn't find it among my bright, shiny paperbacks, but within the pages of an old, worn and very drab-looking volume called *The Promise of the Spirit* by Dr. William Barclay. In scholarly fashion Dr. Barclay explained the role of the Holy Spirit in the Gospels and His place in our lives today. Through constant reference to the Bible he demonstrated that we need the power, guidance and love of the Spirit in order to live in God's way. And it is the Holy Spirit, the communicator between God and man, who brings God and His Son, Jesus Christ, out of the pages of the Bible and into every moment of our daily lives.

Dr. Barclay made it clear beyond all doubt—and here was the key for which I'd been looking so long—that the Spirit is a gift from God, not an achievement to be earned. All my efforts to make myself "worthy," my frantic attempts to "do enough" to gain God's approval, of course they were doomed to failure! I could strain and labor all my life and not be one iota closer to God's goodness and holiness than I was at this moment. To receive the Holy Spirit, Dr. Barclay wrote, all one had to do was ask!

The shining presence of the Spirit, he added, can actually be seen in a person's eyes. Now I knew the secret behind the serene, joyful look I'd caught in so many faces. Perhaps, as the church maintains, I had actually received the Holy Spirit through my confirmation, but I certainly had never appropriated the gift. Now I was finally ready to do so, to ask again in order to know the Spirit of Jesus in my life. I also yearned for that unhampered communication between my spirit and His, and if this meant asking for the gift of tongues, so be it.

Now that I was eager to receive the Holy Spirit, I did not know how to go about it. Even as I was pondering the next step, an announcement was made one Sunday at church: a discussion group on the Holy Spirit was to be held the following Wednesday at the home of a parishioner. I returned home that day with a wonderful feeling about God's timing.

I practically counted the hours of the next three days, anticipation and excitement mounting within me. Although I was certain in my own mind why I was going to the Johnsons' home that Wednesday, it seemed too personal, too inexplicable to share with my family or friends. About two dozen people showed up that night, a few obviously as eager as I, others merely curious or cautious. We gathered in a small living room, most of us sitting on the soft, thick carpet. For what seemed an interminable time to me, we sipped hot coffee from the usual Alaskan mugs, chatted, and sang folk hymns to the accompaniment of several guitars.

Then the room became silent as an Episcopal priest from a nearby community began to talk quietly, simply and unemotionally about the Holy Spirit, and why His presence within each of us was necessary to our Christian lives. He went on in the same clear and concise manner, a "dry Episcopalian" approach which I much appreciated, to explain about speaking in tongues—that it had a very natural, historical place in life in the Spirit. This manifestation had been a definite part of early Christian worship, he said; it was valuable but not essential to our spiritual lives.

The young priest concluded by suggesting that those of us who wanted to ask for the infilling of the Holy Spirit that evening gather downstairs in a recreation room. With several others I followed him down the stairs, feeling that I was entering not a basement but a chapel. This was undoubtedly because of the reverent mood his talk had created, but also the Johnsons had built a small worship area into one end of the big room. Large, well-stuffed pillows lined an altar rail of sorts, and a small wooden cross hung on the plain concrete wall behind.

I sank down on one of the pillows, my eyes on the cross, only vaguely aware of three or four other people kneeling near me. The priest and Mr. Johnson laid their hands on my head, simply asking Jesus to fill me with the Holy Spirit, and to give me the gift of tongues. No bolt of lightning struck, no great emotion overwhelmed me—I felt only an intense quiet in the room.

As I listened to the almost inaudible praying of the people around me I became aware that someone was speaking in what sounded like a fluent oriental language, gentle, musical sounds so beautiful, so prayerful, that I wanted to do the same. And I did, quietly and easily, syllables pouring from me over which I exercised no conscious choice, but which seemed to come from deep within me. I felt as though a great burden was lifting, as if the Spirit within me was at last able to communicate freely with the God above, unencumbered by our own weak and clumsy vocabulary.

Feelings of joy were spilling out, splashing like spring runoff in every direction, and the sense of happiness was so great that I felt like laughing out loud. In the car driving home that night I did, laughing, crying for joy, praising God in my new-found language. This "cloud-nine" state of affairs lasted in fact for several weeks, but it was by no means the most noticeable result of my baptism in the Spirit. What proved to me that He really had come to me in an altogether different way was a new awareness of love—for God and for people. Also a greater love for music and singing, for the Bible, for the beauty of the world around me.

Up till now I'd resented the intrusion of the noisy folk mass style into our traditional Episcopal service. Now I discovered this music was a perfect outlet for my happiness —hand-clapping and "shouting for joy" in the church was irresistible. So was the desire to hug friends and strangers alike. It was as though the Spirit had released me from some lifelong inhibitions so that I could more freely share His love. Community work too, so often a burden, became a joyful offering in the name of the Lord. It was challenging to tackle the myriad problems of the school board, and I even found energy to help start a FISH organization (Friends in Service to Humanity), a volunteer group dedicated to helping people facing emergencies.

With so many evidences of His presence in my life I knew it was time at last to tackle that thorough housecleaning of old fears and anxieties I'd been putting off so long. I'd made a beginning, but the dust and cobwebs still lurking in dark corners would have appalled even the most casual housekeeper. It would not be easy—absolutely impossible, indeed, without the guidance and power of the Holy Spirit—but I knew it could no longer be postponed.

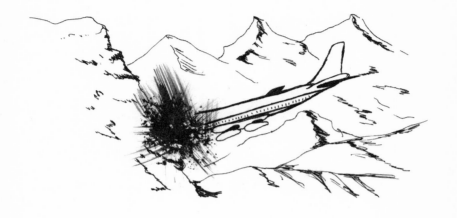

9.

White-Knuckle Flier

Not long after my decision to face up to my fears, I attended a two day Faith-at-Work conference in Anchorage. I found myself in a small "sharing group" along with Heidi Frost, one of the national Faith-at-Work leaders. I cannot remember the topic given us for discussion, I only recall feeling hesitant about opening my inner self to others. One of the members of our group was an airline pilot who talked of the spiritual insights he received while he was in the air. "Insights!" I blurted out in spite of myself. "I'm so terrified when I get into a plane that I can't think at all." Everyone in the room turned to stare at me: next to the pilot I'd probably spent more time in the air than anyone there, and their disbelief was plain to see. "It's just been in the last ten years," I added apologetically. "Since a bad experience."

I felt surprise change to sympathy. For anyone living in Alaska, fear of flying is indeed a crippling problem. In fact it immeasurably complicated my life, since it's almost impossible to move very far from Anchorage without taking to the air. Whenever I visited Fairbanks, Alaska's second largest city, I always went by train, the only railroad route in the state. It took twelve hours, compared to fifty minutes by jet—"a restful change" was my excuse. I even rode the train from California all the way to New York two years in a row, dragging the poor children along. "It's a good education for them," I'd say. "They need to see that there's more than just clouds between us and the East." I found all kinds of reasons to give people, because for many years I'd told no one but Lowell of my disabling fear.

He knew all too well about the weeks of torment I went through before any flight I could not avoid. At night I'd dream of flying into mountainsides or zooming low through the streets of a town, dodging trees and telephone poles. During the day I could not concentrate on my work because I was using all my energies to deal with the D-Day that lay ahead. D for dying—I actually accepted the fact that I was going to die each time I set foot on a plane.

During those miserable weeks of preparation I became a dedicated weather forecaster, clipping maps of frontal systems from the newspapers, and checking temperature and rainfall data of cities along the route. After determining whether the sweeping black line across our path was a stationary or moving front, I'd try to plot where it would be on the day of the flight. I always came to the inevitable conclusion that a gigantic storm system lay directly in the way, and to support my findings the newspaper and radio usually supplied me with timely stories of tornadoes or blizzards.

When D-Day finally arrived, I'd be so nervous I'd have a stomach ache as well as diarrhea. Even the tranquilizers I resorted to were of little help. Poor Lowell had to handle all household and travel details, then literally pull me onto the plane. He had given up long ago trying to convince me of the safety factor in flying. No amount of statistics, no rational argument had any effect on a highly irrational fear.

Once on board I was a basket case, grabbing the arms of my seat, lifting the plane off the ground by myself, worrying about every little cloud that floated by. The moment we were airborne, I had to gulp down two or three Bloody Marys even if it was ten o'clock in the morning. But nothing could stop my heart from pounding right through my chest whenever we hit the slightest bump. I finally realized that it was the turbulence that frightened me the most: even when the air was smooth I could not relax for anticipating the next bump. I thought of a particular ten-hour flight from Tahiti to Los Angeles when everyone on the plane, including most of the crew, had been sound asleep—except me. It was a calm, moonlit night, but I flew that plane every foot of the way.

Along with alcohol and pills, prayer was my other major weapon, but the results up until now had been equally unsatisfactory. My anxiety and tension were a block to any real communication with God, my prayers becoming mere cries of fright. Stumblingly, I related all this to the Faith-at-Work group. Heidi Frost seemed to understand immediately. It was wrong, she said, for me to have to waste so much time and energy in fighting what she called a phobia. "You said this fear began after a bad experience. Did you know bad memories can be healed?" she asked. I had never heard of such a thing. "Would the fear go away then?" "Yes," Heidi stated with great confidence, "but it will take time, just like a broken bone or other injury takes time to heal."

When she suggested that the group pray for such a healing I eagerly assented. She moved my chair to the center of the room while the group formed a circle about me, their hands on my head and shoulders. Heidi then asked me to think back on the incident, trying to remember every detail, particularly my thoughts and feelings at the time, and to tell them all about it. I shut my eyes and went back ten years, for the first time recalling many of the details about that day.

The children and I were flying from Florida to New York on the Pan American executive plane at Dad's disposal. Lowell had flown on ahead in our little Cessna, while I elected to travel in swifter luxury. The plane was a two-engine B-23, not very large, but the interior was as comfortable as a living room, with couches, armchairs and tables instead of monotonous rows of airline seats. We almost filled it, as I recall: Dad and Mother, other family members and guests. The only children were Anne and Dave, who were three and one at the time.

It was an unusually clear day, deep blue skies with not a cloud in sight. Of couse we unfastened our seat belts after takeoff and relaxed around the room. I sat in an armchair at one of the tables, playing cards with my father. Dave was sitting quietly on my lap, enjoying the game as much as we. We were at about nine thousand feet over the Virginia coastline, when suddenly the plane dropped, like a plummeting elevator, straight down several thousand feet.

The descent ended with a shuddering jolt. It came as a total surprise to everyone—we were all flung against the ceiling, cards and glasses flying everywhere. All the others clutched for their seats as they came back down. I had both arms around Dave and didn't dare let go. While the rest landed on soft cushions, I hit the arm of my chair. It was a sharp, hard blow. I felt a stab of pain, then rolled onto my side in agony.

I discovered later that I had broken my coccyx, the small bone at the base of the spine. I had always heard that this was a particularly painful fracture, and now I could verify it. I could not sit down, in fact it would be many months be-

fore I could sit comfortably again, so I moved to the back
of the plane to lie on a small empty couch. The air was
smooth again and once the cabin had been cleaned up, activities returned to normal. The others were laughing and
joking over the silly things that had happened to various
objects during our abrupt descent.

Heidi interrupted me at this point. "What about you?" she
asked. "Wasn't anyone concerned about your injury?" I
thought for a long moment, for the first time realizing that
I had been virtually ignored. "No one seemed aware of it," I
replied at last. "Only the pilot came back to ask if there was
anything he could do to make me more comfortable." He'd
also explained to me that we had passed through a dry
front: a wind shear at that point had caused the clear air
turbulence. Thinking back now, I remembered his attention
with a feeling of deep warmth. I quickly pointed out, however, in defense of my family, that we had been brought up
with the Spartan attitude toward hurt and pain—be brave,
keep a stiff upper lip, ignore it, and it would go away.

For the first time in all those years I remembered suffering in silence, feeling deeply rejected and alone, hurting
inside as well as out. Heidi reaffirmed that those feelings
were undoubtedly intertwined with the fear at the core of
my phobia. She now suggested that I picture Jesus coming
through that blue sky toward the airplane, opening the door
wherever it was, and taking me into His arms.

This was easy to do; I could still visualize every detail of
the inside of that plane, particularly the narrow cushions
where I was trying in vain to find a comfortable position.
The sharp, throbbing pain came back almost as strong as
when I'd first experienced it, as did the hurt I'd felt inside
because no one was giving me the comfort I craved. The
rest of the imagery followed as if it too had actually happened. I could see the door opening, that intense blue sky
beyond, and Jesus moving toward me. I felt His physical
presence as I had known it in the earthquake, and that

same indescribable peace. Then Heidi and the others prayed that Jesus would take away all physical and emotional hurt through His loving concern.

I did not have long to wait before facing my next plane trip, and I was grateful for Heidi's warning about the pace of healing as I felt the usual pre-flight anxiety. Again I had to be shoved on board, but as I clung to my seat during takeoff, I realized that something was different. That intense, soul-deep fear was gone. What I felt now was more like a conditioned reflex of anxiety. I was still tense, but also elated over this beginning of progress. Now I could go to work on the problem: reason prevailed, and so did Jesus, as I began to feel His presence beside me in the air.

The healing of my phobia took almost two years, and I still experience occasional moments of alarm. But I no longer waste energy on worry before a flight, pills and alcohol are not necessary, and I leave weather problems to Jesus. I have yet to relax enough to sleep on an airplane, but I'm sure that this, too, will come, if I am patient and trusting. I marvel at His perfect timing in all things: two winters later, while Anne and Dave remained in junior high school in Anchorage and Lowell was in Juneau at the legislative session, I found myself practically commuting by air between the two cities, over one of the most mountainous, bad-weather routes in the world.

That spring I was invited to attend a week-long Faith-at-Work seminar near Seattle. Five other Alaskans went with me, and I was so absorbed in lively conversation that I completely forgot I was in an airplane. In fact, one of the women had to remind me to fasten my seat belt before we landed!

At the seminar we were again divided into small groups— the sixty participants coming from many western states as well as Canada. This time I felt no shyness, only a new confidence and readiness to make new friends. One of these was a young woman from the Seattle area. Pat Lelvis had been a Lutheran missionary on the Afghan-Pakistan border, and we found we had much to share.

On the second day I told my sharing group of my recent healing experience. Some of the members were obviously dubious, perhaps even embarrassed at my uninhibited baring of personal feelings. Pat, however, seemed deeply interested and asked many questions. Later that day she came to my room and confessed that she too was fighting a crippling fear—of water. She had always been a good swimmer and it had been her favorite sport. However, several years ago she had almost drowned in a heavy surf off the coast of Finland. Pat had been filled with a similar irrational terror ever since, and had made up her mind that she would never swim again. Now she was not so sure. Having heard my story, she believed a bad memory could be healed, and asked if I would pray with her about it.

All my new confidence left me very suddenly. How could I possibly do what Heidi Frost had done for me? And alone. "Help, Lord," I cried silently, as I frantically wondered how to handle this new situation. Then I remembered the women who had come from Alaska with me. Betty Hart and Judy Lethin had both had experience with healing prayer, and they were in rooms just down the hall. "Please, please be in your rooms!" I thought as I told Pat I'd be right back, and rushed away. I found them together, sitting quietly as if they were waiting for me. After explaining the situation as quickly as I could, I led them back to my room.

I had never thought I would be reliving this scene, especially with me in Heidi's position. But there I was, with my hands on Pat's head, asking her to remember every detail of the day she came near drowning. If I had known what we were getting into I'm sure I would never have started.

There were no problems related to Pat's actual experience. But as she relived her feelings at the time she suddenly burst into tears and, sobbing hysterically, started to tell us about the death of her mother, shortly after the swimming incident. It was a heart attack, and Pat had had to watch her mother literally strangle to death. Between racking sobs Pat described how horrible it had been to see her mother gasp-

ing for breath. It was Judy who caught the connection between the two experiences, and she led us in prayer, asking
Jesus to come into both memories, and to reassure Pat that
her mother was now in His radiant presence. At the close,
Pat said she was going to go for a walk in the woods.

When we met for the evening session, Pat had completely
regained her composure. Before we separated for the night,
she thanked me for helping her, remarking that it was the
first time she had actually allowed herself to grieve for her
mother since her death. Nothing more was said until a
couple of days later, when we were given an unexpected
two hours of free time. I needed exercise after so much
sitting, but it was pouring rain outside. Then I remembered
the beautiful indoor pool in the basement of the conference
center. In my usual unthinking fashion, I asked Pat if she
would like to take a swim with me. She replied that she'd
love to, and we headed downstairs. It wasn't until we had
slipped into the warm water and were exclaiming over how
good it felt, that I suddenly remembered Pat's fear. This
time I kept my big mouth shut, and when she said, "Let's
swim some laps," simply stayed close and kept an eye on her.
She seemed perfectly relaxed, however, and swam beautifully. When we finally stopped to catch our breath, she
grinned at me. "Jesus always did know how to calm the
water, didn't He?" she said.

10.

I Give You Lowell and His Airplane

I was standing at the kitchen sink washing dinner dishes as Anne departed with her date. The sun still touched the plants on the window sill although it was nine in the evening. Anne's friend was starting his big motorcycle, the engine shattering the stillness of our woods. Our precious daughter climbed on behind him, perching precariously on the tiny rear seat. Then they sped out our driveway, Anne's long hair flying behind her.

I had combed and braided that dark hair only yesterday,

it seemed, telling her what to do, worrying about her almost constantly. Now she was a young woman in high school, soon to go to college. Fortunately for her and me, I had finally learned to be a far wiser, more trusting mother. "O.K., Jesus," I whispered, "she's in Your hands—thanks for taking care of her."

I had said the same brief prayer an hour earlier when Dave took off in a similar burst of speed and noise. He had just obtained his license and was driving our newly acquired second car, an old one with many rattles and scars, and a broken muffler which to Dave's great delight emitted a loud roar. He was headed for a party with his ski-team crowd, and when I suggested that he keep an eye on the clock, his response was one I heard many times a day. "No sweat, Mom."

Not a bad description. There had been a time, until very recently, when I would have "sweated it out" until both youngsters were safely home again. And I had reacted in the same way toward Lowell from the moment we were married.

I hated to think of the energy I had wasted in anxiety over the years. I remembered the time, just after Dave was born, when Lowell undertook his longest and perhaps most hazardous expedition—sailing on an Arab dhow around the Indian Ocean. Not only was he away for months, but there was no way that we could keep in communication, even via letter. I had seen enough of dhows when I was in the Middle East to know that they remained afloat only through "the grace of Allah." The sole navigational aid was a rudimentary compass, running lights might or might not work depending on oil for the lamps, and I remained in a state of nervous exhaustion the whole time he was gone.

One reason we'd moved to Alaska was that Lowell would not have to take such extensive trips so far from home, but once we were settled in the wilderness state, there seemed to be even more occasions for worry. In the spring of 1962 Lowell decided to make a three-day visit to an Arctic research station on an ice island which literally floated around the North Pole. Arlis II was an especially thick piece of fresh water ice, about two and one-half miles square and fifty feet deep, probably cast off by a coastal glacier. It moved in a giant circle about the pole, taking a couple of years to do so, the motion almost imperceptible in the midst of the salt water pack ice. The research lab at Barrow, in cooperation with the U.S. Navy, was conducting a number of scientific experiments there and Lowell wanted to film their work and life on the island.

Arlis was beyond the range of Lowell's plane, so he hitched a ride with the lab's R4D, a twin-engine support plane which made trips with supplies every three days. They were in their final weeks of work because summer was about to set in, when the island's surface ice would become too soft to land on.

It wasn't until Lowell was en route to the island in the R4D that he learned that the research might have to come to a halt even sooner because Arlis II was drifting swiftly toward Siberia, out of the long-range capability even of the R4D. The plane dropped Lowell off along with food and fuel supplies, and flew back to Barrow. Just before its return trip three days later, mechanics discovered that one of the airplane engines had to be replaced; a new one would have to be sent all the way from California. They radioed the men on the island that there would be a week's delay.

Ten days went by before I was called and told of the hang-up. The project director expected the problem would be solved "in a few days." But another week passed without word and I became more concerned, especially since I couldn't find out the cause of the continuing delay. I worked myself into my usual frenzy of anxiety, and when the third week had passed, at the suggestion of friends I called the Commanding General of the Air Force in Alaska.

The general was most solicitous, and within a short time was able to dig out the true story for me. Unfortunately this only fed my fears—no wonder I had not been told the facts before. Apparently the new engine had somehow become lost between Los Angeles and Barrow (this can only happen in Alaska), and finally had to be reordered. Meanwhile Arlis II was rapidly moving beyond the range of the support plane. I was frantic now, and also fighting a bad cold aggravated no doubt by worry. I tearfully asked the general if there was any way the Air Force could help out. "Only in a medical emergency," he said. I made a mental note to develop pneumonia and stagger into a hospital saying that only my husband's presence could save my life.

In desperation now, I decided to call my father. All my life Dad had seemed like a knight on a white charger to me because he could always perform the impossible, whether it was obtaining a vital airline route for Pan Am or finding friends a hotel room on Waikiki Beach on a holiday weekend. "Please help, Dad," I croaked, feeling closer to pneumonia every minute.

Dad listened sympathetically as always and said he'd call back. Life looked brighter, and my cold felt better. The phone rang a few hours later. "Tay," said Dad in his cheeriest voice, "there are problems involving the use of airplanes now—the question of range, and also rotten summer ice conditions on the island—but don't worry, the Navy says they will probably be able to get to them with an ice-breaker in another month or so." My pneumonia was back.

Unfortunately, my calls for help had alerted the press (even *The New York Times* had a front page story) and when I picked up the local paper the next day, headlines told of five scientists and Lowell drifting on an ice island closer and closer to the Russian coast. A Boston newspaper report, complete with picture of Lowell, speculated "as to whether the U.S. and Russia can achieve a scientific *modus vivendi* in the Arctic area. Specifically, what will the Russian reaction be to the American courier planes that periodically serve the island?" Visions of an emaciated husband in a Siberian prison camp sent me straight to our family doctor. But Rod Wilson only wanted to hear all about Lowell's ex-

citing adventure, and almost forgot to write me out a prescription.

Disappointingly for the newshounds, the story ended as
undramatically as it had begun. In a final supreme effort the
R4D, its new engine installed, was able to reach the island,
make a most precarious landing, an even more hazardous
takeoff, and return Lowell to Anchorage five weeks late, but
safe and sound. In fact, he looked unusually tanned and
rested, having thoroughly enjoyed his stay, taking hikes over
the ice, reading lots of books, sleeping long hours and eating
steak from a well-stocked food supply. The last detail was
too much—the kids and I had subsisted on hot dogs and
TV dinners for the final two weeks. Our bank account had
hit bottom because Lowell had missed several lecture com-
mitments, income we'd been counting on.

As the years passed, Lowell's plane trips into the Alaskan
wilderness, particularly around mountain slopes and glaciers,
continued to be a source of worry for me. I could never (I
still don't) understand why he wanted to fly up onto a
snowy mountainside during the spring or summer when we
had to live with winter conditions for six months a year
anyway.

And then came the July day when his glacier-hopping
buddy, Don Sheldon, asked Lowell to help him fly a group
of climbers off one of the highest peaks in the Alaska Range.
Don was Alaska's most daring and colorful bush pilot, often
flying expeditions into mountain base-camps. Now one of
these parties needed help in getting out quickly—they had
been marooned for many weeks due to exceptionally heavy
snowstorms.

Evacuation Day dawned cloudy but flyable. I kissed
Lowell goodbye about 5:00 a.m., along with my usual "please
be careful," and then tried to keep extra busy throughout the
long day. The clouds descended and it began to rain soon
after he had left, but I tried to console myself with the
thought that he was flying two hours north into the interior

where the climate was drier. By six o'clock that night I was a wreck, and started calling the FAA's Flight Information Service. These busy men are most obliging about giving out light-aircraft arrival information once, but by the third time their patience wears thin.

Late that night, just as I hung up the phone after what I realized had to be the last inquiry, Lowell himself called from Don's headquarters in Talkeetna. "Don't worry, dear," —ha!—"Don and I got most of the party out. I'll spend the night here, and we'll get the rest in the morning." "But," I sputtered, "what about the weather?" "It's not bad," he replied in his usual noncommittal way. "And the forecast is for improvement tomorrow."

What he didn't tell me about their combined rescue efforts that day would have kept me awake in an agony of fear all night long. Apparently Lowell had followed Don about 9:00 a.m. to a slope high up on the steep mountainside where the climbers had tramped out a runway strip of sorts. From photographs I saw later it looked like a short, narrow driveway headed uphill at a 40-degree angle, with the upper end facing a sheer rock precipice. Landing too long was out of the question, and going around to try again equally impossible.

Lowell said that setting the plane down had been "no problem": the climbers had even placed poles along one side of their makeshift runway so that the flyers could gauge their distance from the ground in poor light. It was the taking off that was difficult. Lowell and Don both carried heavy loads on the first trip because there were eight climbers in the party, with tons of heavy gear. The little planes headed downslope to get back into the air, and anyone who has done any mountain flying knows what such a takeoff is like. The plane bounces roughly, the skis chattering on the rough surface for what seems like an eternity, sometimes becoming airborne briefly, only to sink back onto the snow again. When the plane finally gets into the air, it staggers through a maddeningly slow ascent due to the high altitude.

Nevertheless Don and Lowell each made one successful flight out that morning. It was after their return to the slope, while they were waiting for the planes to be loaded again, that the clouds moved in, hiding the peak above. Lowell was growing concerned, but Don, who knew the terrain as well as he knew the layout of his own home, was more confident.

By the time they were ready to go, the clouds had crept in closer, threatening to engulf them completely. Don suggested he take off first, negotiating the tricky gorge with its abrupt 90-degree angle. Lowell readily acquiesced, and elected to wait on the ground until Don radioed him that the narrow pass was still open.

Don took off, his silver Cessna 180 disappearing into clouds almost immediately. Now Lowell was truly alarmed because one simply cannot fly among a jumbled mountain mass with zero visibility, no matter how well one knows the terrain. He decided at that moment that regardless of Don's radio message, he would delay his own takeoff until conditions improved. He was acutely aware of his own limitations in flying this kind of operation and was prepared to stay with the remaining climbers for as long as necessary.

Don, in the meantime, was surprised to find the cloud cover so low on the backside of the slope. He had found himself in the "soup" at the end of his takeoff run, but thought it was a cloud pocket and he would find more open conditions shortly. He continued to fly blind, however, with no safe way of turning back. So he elected to head on down through the mountain gorge, maintaining a straight course (hopefully) between the rock walls, judging that sharp turn ahead according to time and compass.

Only Don's long-time familiarity with the route saved him, and perhaps some kind of intangible, intimate closeness to the mountains he loved. About halfway down the narrow gorge, still totally enveloped by thick clouds, he decided it was time to make that turn to the left. He did, but moments later thought he could detect an almost imperceptible darkening of the white curtain ahead. He instantly banked his plane more sharply to his left. He told Lowell later that he must have come within yards of hitting the mountainside.

A few more minutes of blind flying brought Don out from beneath the cloud layer at dead center in the gorge. The exit route and lower slopes of the mountain could be easily seen ahead. Dripping with perspiration, acutely aware of his extremely close call, Don radioed Lowell. "I think maybe you better stay put," was his laconic message. He added he'd be back as soon as the weather improved.

Lowell was greatly relieved to hear that Don was safe, although he had no idea how close a call his friend had had, and was more than willing to settle in with the climbers for as long as it took the weather to clear. A snowstorm was howling about their tent camp now, and everyone retreated to shelter for some hot lunch.

That evening, just when Lowell had begun preparations to spend the night, he noticed brighter light around them. The snow had stopped falling, and he thought he could begin to see some breaks in the overcast. Within a half an hour, there had been a great improvement, the clouds parting to reveal the peaks bathed in the pink glow of the evening sun.

As Lowell prepared Charlie for takeoff, he heard the far-off drone of Don's engine. The little silver plane was circling overhead within minutes, and it wasn't long before Don was ready to take off with Lowell again. On that trip and the final one the following morning, they encountered no further problems.

When Lowell told me the story of Don's extremely close call, and of his own decision to stay behind until the weather cleared, I realized fully for the very first time that Lowell really was cognizant of the limitations of his airplane and would not be swayed to exceed them. I had to admit to myself that he'd always been cautious about bad-weather flying, despite the pressures of passengers and the excitement of the adventure itself.

It was then that my whole attitude toward his flying began changing. After all, it was not I, but he who was responsible for his conduct. How had I ever put myself in the godlike role of sustaining him in health and safety anyway? Since I was learning to let God be God in other areas of my life, why not with Lowell? Didn't God love Lowell even more than I, if that were possible, and therefore wouldn't He look out for him far better than I possibly could? I was discovering enough about God to know, too, that whatever happened in Lowell's future would be God's plan for me as well.

The day finally came, as I stood near the Anchorage runway watching Lowell's little plane grow smaller and smaller against the mountains, when I said, "All right, God, he's in Your hands now. I know You are watching over him." I did this many times in the months ahead, and gradually, as I persisted, the anxious, controlling reactions to Lowell's activities were replaced with new understanding, gratitude, even enthusiasm.

Seeing the difference this made in Lowell's and my relationship, I knew I would have to do the same with Anne and Dave. They had both long been firmly tied to Mother's apron strings. Now, however, they had reached their teens and were well prepared and ready to break away. Dave, in particular, with his love of the out-of-doors, began to take longer and more ambitious camping trips with his buddies. With the wilderness at our doorstep, they were off almost every weekend in spring and fall, and often for several weeks at a time during the summer.

Dave and his closest friend were particularly interested in the wild animals and birdlife; armed only with binoculars and cameras, they scrambled up the rocky Chugach Mountains after the elusive mountain goat. Or they paddled a canoe down the swift rivers of the Kenai Peninsula, looking for whistling swans, eagles and owls.

Preparations for a two-week pack trip deep into the Chugach National Forest had me fluttering about him like a mother hen. I checked the extra socks and shirts going into his pack, made sure he had plenty of rain gear. He was infinitely patient with me, but when I began questioning him about his food supplies, he'd had enough. "No sweat, Mom. Tim and I are overloaded as it is." And he firmly closed his pack to my prying eyes.

I worried the entire two weeks they were away. It rained hard almost the whole while and I felt guilty lying in my warm, dry bed at night, listening to the downpour on the roof. With each hot meal I prepared I wondered if the boys were chewing on beef jerky and raisins. They arrived back looking healthier than when they'd left, and both declared that they'd never eaten better. (Ouch!)

I continued to worry, however, about bears and moose. The boys never carried a gun, and only laughed when I suggested tying some bells onto their packs. "Then we'd scare away the animals we want to see, Ma."

Fortunately I had turned Dave's life, too, over to God before he spent a summer surrounded by hundreds of bears. He took the Fish and Game Department job, working with spawning salmon, the summer after he graduated from high school. He and another young man spent two months at a cabin on a remote lake in the Canadian wilderness. When I asked a friend who had been there what the place was like, he replied, "Fantastic! A beautiful spot—and you have never seen so many bears!"

A few years earlier that comment would have sent me into a whole summer of frantic hand-wringing. Actually, as with Lowell, it was Dave who had a far more genuine regard for the real dangers of the situation than I did. He didn't need anyone warning him about bears, after almost daily encounters with the huge brownies and grizzlies. And he enjoyed the entire experience so much that he returned the following summer, with no opposition from me.

Anne enjoyed camping and hiking as much as Dave, but did not go as often, or begin as young as he. Still, her first winter expedition sent me into spasms of anxiety. It was the ski team's annual "glacier stampede," several hundred miles north in the Alaska Range. At that time I pictured all glaciers as being criss-crossed with deep half-hidden crevasses, and I cringed at the thought of Anne and her friends clambering over that treacherous ice.

She returned safely, of course, full of enthusiasm over her experience. Her only close call had come when her contact-lens solution froze in the below-zero nighttime temperature. Since her eyesight is poor without glasses, she knew this was a problem, but solved it by placing the bottle under her arm in the sleeping bag. For my benefit, I suspect, she did pose for one snapshot seated high above a yawning crevasse, her fur mukluk-clad feet dangling into the dark depths. Laughing at my look of horror, she proudly hung a blown-up copy on the wall of her room.

Not only did I have the children's wilderness excursions to worry about, I was equally concerned about teenage social life, particularly their driving on our crowded city streets. I was anxious, too, over their exposure to drugs and alcohol, almost as prevalent in our schools as elsewhere. Fortunately for my overactive nerves, however, this was not a particular threat because both Anne and Dave were members of the "jock set," committed to rigorous training for their cross-country skiing and running teams.

I almost worried myself sick, however, over their being out on our icy roads in the almost perpetual nighttime of the Alaskan winter. I'd occasionally ask them to drive me on errands, a kind of sneaky check ride from which I usually emerged a nervous wreck. Then, of course, there was the added worry over how Anne's boy friends drove—I even considered taking check rides with them!

In retrospect, I am ashamed to count the hours I wasted in unproductive anxiety over both children, and deeply thankful that I was finally able to place their lives, as I had Lowell's, in God's hands. I still have a childish habit of taking them back, and worrying as though their well-being depended on my mental exertion. When this happens I try to remind myself of the earthquake: how in that moment when the ground opened beneath us—when no amount of motherly care and forethought could accomplish anything at all—He was there, and we were all three upheld in perfect safety.

He is there so much more literally than I ever give Him credit for! All during the children's growing years, for instance, I saw myself as the all-important instigator and director of, along with everything else, their religious development. I didn't have a great deal to point to for my pains; by the time they reached high school their ski races were interfering with Sunday church, and about the only prayers they volunteered at the dinner table were pleas for fresh snow.

Imagine my surprise, when Anne went to Dartmouth College as a freshman, to learn that she'd become a member of a Christian fellowship group—and without a single hint or shove from Mother! By Christmastime she had made her own personal commitment to Jesus, and in the spring she received her baptism in the Holy Spirit. I do not even know what the dynamics were which led her to Him, only that she responded so much more swiftly and graciously than I had.

Later she told me that when she was confirmed at age twelve by Bishop Gordon, she felt a strong electrifying presence, but did not understand what it was. Now she believes that at that moment she experienced the inpouring of the Holy Spirit. And during her teens I'd worried interminably about her "finding God!" He'd been at work all the while, silently, secretly, sovereignly. How much I needed to become aware of this in every area of our lives!

11.

"Ladies and Gentlemen . . ."

It was a hot, sunny afternoon in June, 1945, the kind that everyone hopes for on Graduation Day. On the small, crowded stage, however, the air was stifling and I wondered for a moment if I might faint. If I did, I thought hopefully, I would get out of the ordeal ahead of me.

I had known, ever since the spring of my junior year in high school when I was elected president of the student body, that I would have to speak at the commencement exercises, the traditional presentation of the gavel to the incoming president. The brief ceremony required only a few words, but the thought of saying anything at all in front of a large group of people terrified me. My dread of the event had grown through the months until, now that the moment was here, I was almost literally paralyzed by fear.

Our class was sitting in three rows on the stage, facing a sea of faces filling the large gymnasium. I searched the crowd for my mother and father, then found them with the rest of the family at the very front, almost filling a whole row. I wanted so badly to give a smooth flawless speech for my proud, smiling parents, who confidently expected this of me. But how could I? I knew I was going to disgrace myself —my knees were already shaking and my mouth felt so dry that I wondered how I'd ever get my tongue to move.

I thought of all the other graduations I had attended in this gym, from the time I had sat as a first-grader with the lower-school body there to the left of the stage. The graduating seniors with their long white dresses and floral bouquets had looked like angels—exquisitely perfect creatures far removed from me. Even when I moved to the upper-class bleachers on the right, seniors had still seemed to me superior beings, beyond my reach in every way.

During my years in the upper school, Mother was chairman of the Board of Trustees, and therefore gave a talk at each graduation ceremony. Always poised and confident, she read her remarks from the podium in a clear, polished, professional way. When I entered my senior year she'd resigned her position. "Two Pryors on one platform would be too much," she told me affectionately. "Now it will be your turn to speak." My heart flipflopped at the very thought. Did everyone else there that day expect me to do as well as Mother?

The principal was smiling at me. Somehow I'd missed her words of introduction. Waves of panic swept over me as I stood up, almost falling over my long skirt on my way to the front of the stage. Then I recalled with horror that I had placed the gavel beneath my seat. I went back and groped about the floor, the rose stems I was clutching scratching my arms, the waiting silence almost suffocating me.

I found the gavel, dropped the bouquet, and turned to find the junior who was the incoming president waiting for me. She looked poised and beautiful in her long pastel gown and I rushed toward her, thinking I might just hand her the gavel with a big smile, then retreat to the security of my chair.

No, I knew I could not do that—not after having spent weeks memorizing the eight sentences of my short speech. I was caught, standing there center stage, hundreds of pairs of eyes expectantly on me.

I was shaking so hard I could barely stand, and when I finally managed to open my glued-together lips, I could hear a high, quivering sound that must have been my voice. Somehow the first few words slipped out—all that memorizing had at least produced that much. But the next sentence faded into nothing. I stood there, my mouth still open, my mind a total blank. The ghastly silence seemed to stretch on forever. Finally I found the wits to turn around and flee back to my chair. I had failed, as I knew I would, and at that moment I made a solemn vow never again to speak in public.

In 1968, with Anne in junior high school and Dave in sixth grade, I became concerned with the way Alaska's public schools stacked up against other states in preparing students for college. I followed the decisions of our local school board closely, longing to be involved, but lacking the nerve to make a move. Politics was fine for Lowell, but the idea of me running for an elective office was beyond the realm of reality.

Then a friend made up my mind for me, handing me a petition already filled out with all the required information and signatures. I took a deep breath, slipped into the Borough Clerk's office and left it on her desk. Fortunately for me the great furor over school boards had not yet begun; there was little interest in the race that year and I was elected, largely due to Lowell's name, I'm sure.

I had to speak at just one public meeting that year, and then only for five minutes, but I almost worried myself sick for days beforehand. By this point in my life I was learning to take every concern to God, and He came to my rescue in dramatic fashion. A few hours before my talk I bent over to pick something up and stabbed my eye with the edge of a notebook, injuring it enough to warrant seeing a doctor. He was concerned over possible complications and covered it with an elaborate bandage which swathed my whole head. So I faced what might have been a hostile teachers' audience that night bandaged like a veteran, one-eyed and weak, but smiling. When I apologized for being unprepared, I could feel sympathy flowing toward me. I was able to escape unscathed after saying only a few sentences.

But obviously God was not going to leave me there, defeated by a fear, dodging around a problem instead of facing it squarely. And the problem, as I thought and prayed over it in the following months, seemed to center around my very low self-opinion. I knew the Bible told us to love ourselves along with our neighbors—but how could you do it? You knew yourself too well! How could you be aware of all the mean, selfish, stupid things you'd done and even tolerate yourself?

Because God loved you and forgave you. I knew with my mind that that was the answer; during the battle with sleeping pills I'd even begun to sense it inside. Then came the baptism in the Holy Spirit, and I was even surer of it. God must love me very much to fill me with His own Spirit—how could I go on hating what He loved?

It was about this time that I had a dream, such a powerful and vivid one that I still remember every detail. I dreamed that I was among a group of people acting in a play. We were wearing costumes, and walked onto a stage before blinding lights. Jesus was there, standing between us and the audience. We stopped at an altar in the middle of the stage; He stood in front of it while we faced Him from behind. I started to take off my costume, which included a mask. Now I could see His face clearly: He was looking sternly into my eyes, obviously annoyed that I was taking so long to shed my disguise. I suddenly wanted to hurry as fast as possible, and simply tore the mask and costume off, then rushed around the altar to join Him. I debated whether to stop and kneel, but instead decided to go straight to Him. I looked at His face again and now He was smiling at me. He stretched out His hands and took mine. Then we walked off the stage together.

I puzzled for a long time over the symbolism of the stage and the altar. But the central message of the dream seemed clear: Jesus wanted me—loved me!—just as I was, without any effort to conceal my true self or appear like someone else. He loved me, Tay Thomas, shortcomings and all, and with this incredible realization my confidence began to grow until I was taking on tasks I would never have dreamed of trying before.

I continued to draw the line, however, at public speaking. I thought of that as a gift, and certainly not mine. I've known many individuals, like my mother and Lowell, who thrive on speaking before crowds. The larger the audience, the better Lowell likes it; he never gropes for words, but expresses himself succinctly and entertainingly. Obviously this undertaking should be left to the people with this particular talent.

With my high school graduation debacle indelibly imprinted on my mind I determined that I would try to serve the Lord through my daily living, and perhaps also with my pen, but never the spoken word. Which is why I was utterly unprepared, when the principal of the West Anchorage High School phoned me in 1974 and invited me to be their principal graduation speaker, to hear my own voice answer, "Yes I'd love to." I hung up the phone, wondering what in the world had gotten into me. My throat was already gravel-dry as I pictured the thousands of people packed into that auditorium each year when I handed out diplomas for the school board. That was frightening enough, even though no words were required. But to give the evening's main address —the very thought turned me into a quivering mass of anxious knots, and I still had two weeks to go.

The first seven days were one tormented nightmare as I wrestled with what looked like an impossible situation. One day, at the end of that week, I decided it might help if I wrote out the speech and, with pencil and paper in front of me, I spent some time in prayer. No inspiration came. At last I picked up *Good News for Modern Man*, a colloquial translation of the New Testament which I loved, and after asking the Holy Spirit for guidance, opened the pages to what I prayed would be a helpful passage. As my eyes fell on the words in the fourteenth chapter of First Corinthians I almost dropped the Book:

> Set your hearts on spiritual gifts, especially the gift of speaking God's message . . . the one who speaks God's message speaks to men, and gives them help, encouragement and comfort.
>
> 1 Corinthians 14:1, 3, TEV

When I'd recovered a little from the bull's-eye quality of the verse, I studied it more carefully. The key to making a speech, it seemed to be saying, was to place my attention not on myself but on the people God was trying to reach, and on the help, encouragement and comfort He had for them. Maybe, I thought suddenly, this was one reason why loving ourselves was so important. Maybe until we truly accepted ourselves we couldn't forget about ourselves, couldn't stop focusing on our own inadequacies and problems, in order to turn outward to others.

Others . . . young men and women who for the past twelve years had been preparing for this night, and now faced a complex, bewildering and terrifying world. Surely no one needed help, encouragement and comfort more than they did. I grabbed my pencil and began to write.

That was an extra-special graduation night for me. I felt no nervousness at all, only an eagerness to share what I knew someone, maybe many in that crowded hall, needed to hear. I talked without embarrassment because I felt I had a message, God's message, to relay. And it must have been heard by at least a few people because the local newspaper commented on it in a rare editorial of praise. Although I had not used them in my talk, the words the reporter chose were "encouragement and comfort."

After the graduation talk I flew east (I can say that so nonchalantly now!) to visit Anne who was taking a summer term at Dartmouth. I bubbled over to her about the ease and self-confidence with which I had faced that crowd. "I really do think I've gotten over all those old insecurities," I said. "I just hope," I added piously, "that the Lord keeps me humble now." Anne grinned at me, "Oh, He will, Mom, He will."

The next day, Saturday, I walked to the Hanover supermarket to buy some food for a party in Anne's dorm that night. I had run out of cash and the banks were closed, but I had my checkbook—I used checks for everything in Alaska. When I wheeled my overflowing grocery cart up to the check-out counter, I said confidently to the girl, "I hope you don't mind taking an out-of-town check." She looked alarmed. "Oh, I couldn't do that, I might lose my job." A line had formed behind me, all ears.

Seeing my bewilderment the girl asked, "How far out of town?" I whispered, "Anchorage, Alaska." "Alaska!" she yelped. "I really would be fired." Turning to the next customer she dismissed me with, "You'll have to see the manager."

He was already on his way over, a tall gaunt New Englander with a look of sour apples on his face. He said nothing, but silently started taking my groceries out of the cart. Flushing with embarrassment, I stammered that my daughter went to college there. "Dartmouth kids are the worst of all," he said. Apparently some students passing bad checks were the cause of this man's bitterness.

"But I've got plenty of identification!" I fumbled in my purse for proofs of my newly-found self-esteem. "I'm a member of Alaska's Land Use Planning Commission and I'm on the Anchorage school board and my husband is a state senator!" The manager went right on collecting groceries. The line behind me had tripled now and I could sense the tears coming fast. "Well—could you, would you please leave my food here until I can borrow money to pay for it?" He nodded curtly, and I rushed from the store crying like a child as I took the least-traveled streets back to Anne's room. Just before I reached the dorm, I remembered her prediction the day before. I started to laugh, the tears still pouring down: "I guess I don't have to worry about humility, Lord! You'll never let us forget where real confidence comes from . . ."

12.

My Secret Garden

As Lowell's and my lives became more and more filled with activity, I found it increasingly hard to escape to some serene spot out of doors for prayerful thought. There was no time for weekends at Birchwood, or even an hour alone in our woods. When I mentioned this difficulty to a friend at St. Mary's, Mary Eddy commented that it wasn't necessary actually to return physically to some peaceful location, so long as we kept the image of it in our minds. "Select some favorite place from your memory," she suggested, "and then envision meeting Jesus there."

I liked her idea, and embarked at once on weeks of mental travel, revisiting romantic spots far removed from committee meetings and school budget deadlines. I almost did not make it beyond the islands of the Pacific because sapphire-blue water, a white beach fringed with palm trees, and hot sun come awfully close to my vision of paradise. I meandered slowly from the Hawaiian Islands to Tahiti, Samoa, Fiji. Bliss. But how to choose which one? I continued on through Australia, up to Thailand and Burma, then across India, Afghanistan, Iran, the Middle East. Again I got hung up over the beaches of Muscat and Bahrain, but I made myself move down through Africa, then Europe, South America, the United States, including our own beautiful state of Alaska.

What a hard decision! But oddly enough, the spot that kept coming back to mind was a small sunken garden behind the house of my childhood. Little used and out of sight, it was often neglected by our elderly gardener. Old Tom made sure the front and back lawns were immaculate and Mother's large vegetable plot well weeded, but this spot was seldom visited and it became a kind of secret place to me, one I retreated to when I lost track of the joys of having three younger brothers and a sister.

It was odd, however, that each time I pictured it now, it seemed to be wintertime. I tried to visualize the garden at other seasons of the year, especially spring and summer. But the rectangular flower beds in my mind's eye remained bare mounds of dirt, the grass on the path brown. Dead leaves were blowing about and the shrubs were wrapped in heavy burlap.

There was a sense of privacy and peace about the place that kept drawing me there. When I shut our bedroom door, knelt by the bed and closed my eyes, it was easy to picture Jesus sitting on the flagstone steps at the far end of that garden. I mentally placed myself at the opposite end, kneeling at a stone bench in the corner. I had found my retreat, although I surprised myself by my own choice, and as the months went by, I found an ever-closer relationship with Him in this garden. I received the answers to many prayers there, and began to learn much about Jesus through His ways of responding to me. His words were few—perhaps only one or two—and often spoken with a gentle, almost chiding humor, as though I were a small, rather stubborn child. But always I felt an overwhelming love in His presence.

One time I was fighting an earache, the remnant of a cold. I was about to take a plane from Juneau to Anchorage and I knew that flying with a plugged-up ear could end in torture. I had become convinced that Jesus could heal today just as He had in Biblical times—I had seen it happen to friends, and had read of miracles occurring to others. And so as I went about my daily routine I prayed for the healing of my ear. But the throbbing grew worse and at last I retreated to my winter garden. "Jesus," I pleaded, kneeling at the stone bench, "it's just an earache, but would You heal it for me?" I could almost feel His hand upon my ear, and peace replace the tension about it. The pain disappeared instantly and never returned, although the ear was still clogged up when the plane climbed over thirty-five thousand feet the next day.

The picture of my mental garden never changed, no matter how often I used it, until I experienced the dream in which I felt Christ's acceptance so deeply—when at His insistence I removed the mask and the disguise. From then on I no longer saw myself kneeling at the bench so far away; my new confidence permitted me to walk down the path and sit on the steps beside Him, and to look Him in the eyes, rather than keeping my head bowed as I had done before.

It was about this time that I traveled to that Faith-at-Work conference near Seattle. And there I had an experience which to this day I do not understand. I cannot explain what happened. I can only describe it.

The conference was held at the Issaquah Convention Center, in a former Catholic convent built by the Sisters of

Providence in 1961 and now leased to the State of Washington. The mammoth gray-stone building itself reminded me of some large manor home in England, particularly the great stone arch curving above the entranceway. The grounds were equally stately and beautiful—lush green lawns sloping down the hillside in all directions towards a thick evergreen forest.

We had little time to enjoy the out-of-doors, however, as we were kept hard at work from early morning until late at night. We had one "walk break" each day, from 10:30 a.m. until lunch at noon, and its purpose was not recreation alone, but to provide us with an opportunity to talk alone with another conference participant outside our "sharing group." It reminded me of high school parties and the excitement of filling out dance cards, as we all rushed about, scheduling a walk on a certain day with someone we especially wanted to talk with. The five conference leaders were in particular demand, so I decided to try first for Carrie Gardiner, one of the staff members from the East Coast, whose deep faith shone like a light from her face. Obviously many others felt the same about her, and although I approached her as quickly as possible, she had only one morning free, the final day.

I looked forward to this particular walk all week, and on Friday it was a joy to wake up to a sunny spring day. We even left our coats behind as we crossed the lawn and walked down a wooded path to one of the only two roads in the area. At first I was aware of other couples strolling by, but by the time we'd reached the road I'd lost track of everything except our conversation.

As we talked, we came to a clearing among the pine trees that lined the road. For an instant I was reminded of a scene from Walt Disney's *Snow White and the Seven Dwarfs*— shafts of sunlight piercing the tall, dark trees to fall on the little glade. There was a small stone house at the edge of the clearing, and I was delighted to note that it was a miniature replica of the conference building, complete with stone arch.

A black-surfaced driveway curved around in front of it, and within that semicircle was the loveliest spring garden I'd ever seen.

As we both stood admiring the beauty before us, we noticed a nun standing by a wheelbarrow on the tarmac. She was wearing a traditional long black habit, her coif hanging to her shoulders, although the handful of nuns still housed at Issaquah were all in contemporary dress. A large man's glove on her left hand was the only indication that she was actually working in the garden.

She waved to us, calling "Come on in!" As we went eagerly over to her Carrie remarked that she herself was an avid gardener and liked nothing better than swapping recipes for mulch and fertilizer. I loved gardening, too, but after a six-month Alaskan winter I simply wanted to stare at the beautiful blooms.

The nun greeted us in a most friendly, welcoming manner. Her face was unlined and her eyes bright and dancing with life, yet we both sensed that she was an elderly person. Carrie asked whether she actually took care of the garden herself. "Oh, I do," she replied. "I spend about three hours here a day." When I asked her if she had always lived in the Seattle area she laughed gaily, saying, "Of course!"

Carrie and the sister then engaged in a lively gardeners' conversation about the dirt mixture in the wheelbarrow and the nun's compost pile. Meanwhile, I wandered about the little garden, noticing the unbelievable tidiness—not a twig or a branch, not even a dead leaf on the ground—the well-pruned bushes, the perfect symmetry of the flower beds and paths. Following one of the latter around some small evergreen trees, I came upon a white marble statue of the Virgin Mary and a small stone seat nearby.

It was the flowers, however, that really caught my attention. Other than a mass of miniature grape hyacinths in a border along the drive, I noticed something odd. There was only one plant of each of the other varieties. I remember clearly a large, lone daffodil, like a bright spot of sunshine.

Other buds came from its stalk—that was something I never remembered seeing either, a single daffodil with many flowers—but only the one was in bloom. The same was true of a tulip nearby, a huge pink blossom, surrounded by many buds. A few steps away was a solitary forsythia bush, its gracefully curving branches a glory of brilliant yellow. And at its base, one vibrant red primrose seemed to shimmer in its own light. These colors, accented by the green bushes behind them, were such exquisite hues that I felt like a thirsty animal—I could not drink enough of their beauty.

As I strolled from flower to flower, I noticed, at the back of the clearing, two straight rows of stout wooden stakes. I asked the sister what they were for, and she smiled. "That will be my summer garden," she said, "dahlias and gladiolas." I felt a great longing to see the garden at that season too, and then time crept back to mind; both Carrie and I realized that our free period must be almost over. We said goodbye reluctantly to our gardener friend, and she told us warmly to come again any time. From the road we both turned back for one more look at the hauntingly lovely scene.

As Carrie and I hurried toward the conference center we overtook another couple and Carrie asked them if they had seen the beautiful garden a short way back. Neither of them had, but there was no time now to turn around. At the main building Carrie and I slipped into the quiet chapel for a moment of prayer together. As we lingered there, reluctant to join the bustle of the food line, on impulse I told her about my interior prayer garden, how I visited it in my mind whenever I wanted to feel the presence of Jesus. In response to her eager questions I described the setting in detail to her. She seemed delighted with the idea, and asked if I would share it with her; she too, she said, desperately needed a place of peaceful refuge.

Flying back to Alaska the next day, I sat beside my friend Mary Eddy. She had been one of the five conference leaders, and wanted to thank me, she said, for helping Carrie so much the day before. "Whatever did you do," she asked, "to give her such a lift?" I was dumfounded. "I didn't do anything," I said, "Carrie helped me, I didn't help her!"

But Mary insisted that I had. Carrie had come to her early Friday morning saying she didn't think she could make it through the day; she was utterly drained from the demands of the week. Mary asked whom she was walking with that morning and when Carrie mentioned me, Mary tried to find me to alert me to Carrie's exhaustion. Thank heaven she didn't succeed! Had I known of Carrie's great need, I would undoubtedly have fallen flat on my face in my typical clumsy attempts to help someone.

I told Mary that all we'd done was talk a little about the power of Christian love, and then spend the rest of the time visiting the nun's lovely garden. Now it was Mary's turn to look stunned. "What garden?" she asked. She had walked along every foot of those two roads all week long and had never seen any garden. Baffled, I got up and walked down the aisle of the plane to ask each of the other Alaskans if they had seen the little clearing by the road with the miniature replica of the conference center. None had, although each one had walked throughout the area every day. I was becoming more and more mystified. From home I wrote a number of the other participants, always receiving the same puzzled reply: What garden?

I finally wrote to Carrie, describing the garden in detail, asking her if she remembered it the same way. "Do you have this same memory, Carrie? Do you remember precisely where it was, and how we got there? Half of me says we may have been led to our own special garden, perhaps cared for by an angel—a garden that may not really exist. The other half says it's actually there but that other walkers were too involved with their discussions to notice it. Perhaps you and I were led to it for a purpose—our own secret garden, but in bloom, and beautiful, not the dead, wintry one that exists in my mind, the one you wanted to share."

I received her reply almost immediately, on stationery covered with flowers:

I love the mystery of the garden, but I saw exactly what you saw! In any event, I was blessed by it and by you that day. Mary is absolutely right about my feeling drained— and then filled. . . . I wish I could describe my own pic- ture of "our" garden—or better yet, paint it. Both are beyond me, but it was a semicircle of trees in the woods . . .

Determined now to settle the matter, I got in touch with my Seattle friend, Pat Lelvis. Pat telephoned the conference center and talked to two people who had worked there a number of years. Both denied the existence of any such house or garden. Then a sister came to the phone, one who had lived there since the house was built in 1961. There had never been any other building on the property except the main house, she stated positively, nor could she remember a nun ever keeping a garden—certainly no one was doing so now. Pat eventually went back to Issaquah herself and combed the area I'd described. She found nothing but some Stations of the Cross in the woods behind the center, aban- doned and half covered with wild growth.

Why Carrie and I should have been vouchsafed this glimpse of another reality, I cannot imagine. The fact that we saw it together was like an underlining of the experience, an insistence that it was, in fact, real, although in what sense I don't begin to understand. I've thought at length about each detail of what we saw. The many buds on a single stalk, for example. Could this be a symbol of our life in the Spirit? Perhaps the gifts He gives us are like these radiant blooms; each time we put one to use in His service perhaps another bud opens into glorious flower.

One discovery I made that day I am sure about. When God uses us to help others there is no strain, no self-conscious scrambling to accomplish things for Him. I thought back to the months following my initial commitment, when I won- dered how Christians found the energy to do all they did. Now I had a clue: I had not even been aware, that Friday morning, that I was helping someone. Quite the contrary, I was conscious only of being helped, of energy flowing into me. By being—for once!—in the place where God wanted me, and at His moment, I finished the "task" He gave me more refreshed than when I began.

This insight helped me become more sensitive to the times and places where God wanted me to work. And then in the summer of 1974 I found myself entering a period of almost non-stop pressure. Lowell's close friend in the state legislature, Jay Hammond, had decided to run for governor, and asked Lowell to enter the race for lieutenant governor. We both admired Jay for his integrity and idealism, and the challenge of running with him and, if elected, working with him to achieve goals they both believed in, quickly won Lowell over.

From that moment of decision, our days for five months were crowded with campaign activities from early in the morning until late at night. We were up against almost overwhelming odds. Jay was known to only two percent of the voters at the beginning of July, and the party organization itself, the business establishment, the state's largest newspaper and organized labor were all strongly opposed to him. To all of them Jay was an unknown, bearded, fisherman conservationist from a rural Eskimo village. To many young and independent voters, however, he represented a new face, a man without ties to any special interest group, and a deep concern for controlled growth in Alaska.

Jay's charisma, Lowell's long-time popularity, combined with hard work and an intensive, old-fashioned door-to-door campaign, turned the tide, and in August Jay and Lowell won the Republican primary. Our job had only begun, however; in the November election we would be facing a well-entrenched opponent who had been governor for two terms, was well-financed and solidly supported by the Teamsters Union, all-powerful in Alaska because of the oil pipeline project. The most difficult aspect of the election was the barrage of devious mud-slinging tactics we had to face, the worst ever seen in our state. I thought that, as a campaign veteran, I could handle malicious half-truths and insinuations, but it was terribly hard on us all, and the excitement of the primary dissolved into grim determination not to retaliate in kind during the final weeks.

We lost ground steadily, however, and on election day, with the race looking like a tossup, I spent the waiting hours scrubbing our house from top to bottom, my usual procedure at such times. It wouldn't have been so bad if the race had been decided by late that evening, in normal fashion. Nothing was settled, though, as the two men remained in a virtual tie all night long, throughout the following day and for three long agonizing weeks afterwards. First one and then the other would pull ahead as votes straggled in. In Alaska paper ballots are still used everywhere except in the major cities, so the counting is slow, results from isolated villages taking days to be tabulated.

Absentee ballots are not counted until a week after the election, and by then, with a slim three-hundred-vote lead, we had to take elaborate precautions against irregularities in opening this mail vote. When the final tally still showed Jay ahead by only a few hundred votes, there had to be an automatic recount of the paper ballots. Another three days in an agony of suspense. The result was still in our favor, although a second recount showed our margin steadily decreasing. The governor, in a final dramatic moment, demanded a third recount.

By now I had lost all hope, as well as the composure I had kept for so long. I could not even pray rationally; all I could do was cry, "Lord, why? Why, after months of such tremendous effort, couldn't we at least have known one way or another on election night?"

On the morning when the governor requested the third recount, I went into our bedroom, closed the door and sank down on my knees. After a few moments I was able to picture myself in my little sunken garden. (Ever since that visit with the nun in the woods, I had seen my childhood garden not in winter but in glorious springtime.) "Please, Jesus," I prayed now, "tell me how this is all going to end. I don't

care now if we win or lose, but please stop this awful uncertainty." I then deliberately pushed all thoughts from my
mind and concentrated on trying to picture His face, His
figure sitting on the steps.

How odd, I thought, I can't visualize Him at all. No verbal
answer to my prayer came either. Several long moments
went by and suddenly a picture did form in my mind, but
only of a shoulder—very clearly only a shoulder, no matter
how hard I tried to envision more. Then it vanished abruptly
and I could not recapture even that much. The message
dawned on me, and I sat back in amazement. What a clear
concise way of telling me to leave everything on His strong
shoulder! I was not to fret or concern myself in any way,
but to delight in total dependence on Him. Shedding all
worry and tension about the election, I concentrated on long
neglected housework and did not give the future another
thought. Three days later we learned that Jay and Lowell
had won by 275 votes.

I'd been so wrapped up in the campaign that I'd scarcely
thought about the fact that victory would mean moving to
Juneau. Once again we faced the decision of where to live.
An apartment for any length of time was out of the question
for Lowell; he'd grown up on a farm and had a terrible time
adjusting to the togetherness of condominiums and high-
rises. Homes were scarce in the Juneau area, however, and
the price tag on the few that were for sale prohibitive.

So we purchased an unspoiled woodsy lot on Douglas
Island, linked by bridge to Juneau, and once again set about
the business of building a home. By buying a package house,
doing our own contracting and much of the interior work,
we figured we could keep the cost to a minimum.

With Lowell settling into his new job as lieutenant governor, however, it soon became apparent that the day-in,
day-out work would have to be supervised by me. How
glad I was now for the years spent learning to depend on
Jesus! Lowell was fairly good with a hammer and saw, but
I couldn't even hang a picture. I felt strongly, however, that

our beautiful stand of pine and alders belonged to the Lord; the house would be His, too. I confidently placed the entire undertaking in His hands, asking Him to be Foreman and Head Carpenter.

The first test came with the man who was to put in our foundation. It had to be extra strong because of poor soil conditions, a large job we had not expected. He was an authoritative take-charge type and, with a sweep of his hand across our lovely lot, indicated that he would have to bulldoze almost to the property line. My arguments turned to chaff in the whirlwind of his expertise. "Jesus," I asked silently, "will You take over?" Early the next morning the foundation man called to say he had studied the lot more carefully and decided he only needed to clear the portion right around the house.

With everything ready to go, I took off with the children for a visit with my parents whom I had not seen since the election. When I called Lowell in Juneau to see how the foundation was coming, he said, "Sit down, you won't believe this." I listened eagerly to hear what miracle God had wrought. Then came the most fantastic story about a barge with a giant hoist running into the channel bridge in the middle of the night, causing enough damage that no heavy traffic would be allowed across until repairs could be made —at least two weeks. I collapsed into a chair. The bridge was the one link between Juneau and Douglas Island, and the only route for the cement trucks and other construction supplies. "Why, Lord?" I thought. "Why such a fluky accident at this particular time?"

I called again just before returning home, quite confident that the foundation would be underway at last. "Well, you won't believe it, but—" Lowell started in, and this time I sank into the chair in advance. Apparently the bridge was useable now, but when the foundation man was ready for the crane, it broke down and they had to send to Seattle for a new part. Another two-week delay. I decided it was about time I got home—obviously Jesus needed me at His side.

I arrived back in time to watch the cement being poured for the basement footings on July 3rd, one month behind schedule. And at once realized that it would have been impossible to start building a moment earlier. Jesus hadn't needed me there; I would only have been in the way! Our original arrangements for someone to put up the exterior frame had fallen through, and no one else had been available all month. It just "happened" that as of July 3rd a highly efficient three-man crew, working exclusively on such package exteriors, was through with a job and willing to come to Juneau.

Walt, Ike and Dan appeared just as we finished unloading the materials. Walt, the head man, sporting shoulder-length hair and a long bushy beard, took right over. The High Time Builders, as they called themselves, worked in their quiet methodical way for two weeks straight, often until eight or nine at night. I never heard a harsh word between them, or even a raised voice, and it was a joy to watch such good work done so fast.

We were blessed by a hot sun the entire time. The thermometer hit 90 degrees one day, breaking the all-time record and sending most of the population to the beaches. It was a rare weather break for Juneau, and the customary rain began to fall just as the roofing was being hammered on. "Perfect timing, Lord," I thought, as I checked for drips so that I could locate leaks for the men on the roof. Next day Walt and his crew moved on to their next job, or back into the pages of the Old Testament, I thought as I watched their bearded faces smiling from the airplane door.

We could hardly believe it as we worked at the beautiful rough-cedar house fitting onto our sloping lot as if they were made for each other. The view from the main floor was spectacular—the blue Gastineau Channel at our feet, the town of Juneau creeping up the mountainside just across the water. It would be a delight living here—if we ever got it finished.

The hardest part was coordinating the various sub-contractors. The city inspector insisted, for instance, that I get the electrician, the plumber and the excavator to the site the same afternoon so that he could give his final O.K. on the hook-up to city power and water. After much telephoning and driving frantically all over town, I rounded up the first two men but not the excavator. When I finally found him, digging up a grocery store parking lot, he told me he couldn't possibly get away that day. At that point I burst into tears. I'm sure the flustered man had never faced a crying contractor before. He hastily agreed to come over for a few minutes.

When we tackled the finish work, communicating with Jesus became a moment-by-moment operation. The only thing I knew about a hammer was how to hit my finger, but I decided we could not spend several thousand dollars on custom kitchen cabinets. Instead I bought a do-it-yourself kit. Two weeks, three glue bottles and twelve off-kilter cabinets later, I was ready for a sanitarium, and well aware that it never would have been done at all if our Head Carpenter hadn't guided every nail and screw. Fortunately several layers of bright paint covered most of my errors.

Wallpapering too required prayer without ceasing. But the geatest challenge of all was laying bricks for the fireplace. When I inquired about tools and mortar at the hardware store, they looked at me as though I were mad. By then I'd acquired quite a reputation about the small town as that female who thinks she's a builder. Their attitude made me even more determined, and I borrowed a formidable book about masonry from the library. "Lord," I prayed, "You've really got to take over now!" And of course it worked—the bricks held, the mortar hardened, the fireplace draws beautifully.

The biggest coup for our Foreman, however, was locating our lost formica. The roll was due to arrive from Anchorage by air freight. But when I told Lowell the formica would be delivered the following morning for sure, because it was on a nonstop flight, he only laughed. "You don't know that airline." Sure enough, when I called in, no one had seen any sign of the formica. "But it's a huge roll," I wailed, "How could it get lost between here and Anchorage on a nonstop flight?" There was an embarrassed silence, then the young man volunteered to check the stops after Juneau—Sitka, Ketchikan and Seattle. "It could be in Tokyo," muttered Lowell.

A day and a half later, after more calls from me, the weary man said, "Lady, I've checked all points three times and nobody's seen it." And so—belatedly—I turned the whole snarl-up over to Jesus, leaving it in His hands where it belonged in the first place. I would not call the airline again until the formica was found and they called me. At lunchtime the next afternoon the telephone rang. "Mrs. Thomas," said the young man, "I don't understand this, but someone just rolled a baggage cart in with your formica on it." He sounded relieved, and puzzled as well. "I can't tell you where it came from—out of the blue, I guess, because no planes have come in since early this morning." Out of the blue is right, I thought: Thank You Lord!

I was painting some window trim that September when I overheard Lowell say, as he put down a door threshold, "Boy, just fits! Perfect!" That's the story of this house, I thought. Every piece has fit—workers, weather, even physical items like furniture and rugs. Fit was particularly close and critical with the bathtub and stove, but they slid into their places like fingers in a glove. The Head Architect knew what He was doing all the way!

The best result of depending on Jesus for every detail was accomplishing it all with a minimum of anxiety. If anyone had told me, the original worrier, a few years ago, that I could supervise the building of a house from pouring the concrete to hanging the curtains without developing peptic ulcers, I would have thought he was crazy. But I was

learning, and the biggest discovery of all came the day before we moved into our newly finished home. The electrical
inspector had told me to have someone fill in the trench
over the power line into the house. That someone, of course,
was me.

I had been warned to keep rocks away from the connection, but as I strained to lift shovelsful of the heavy dirt, I
could see that it was loaded with stones of all sizes. If I
picked them all out there would be little left, I thought
wearily, and I'd be in that ditch all day. I leaned on my
shovel for a few moments, painfully aware of my blistered
hands, the dirt in my hair, my muddy work clothes. Then I
straightened my aching muscles and looked up at the house
we had succeeded in building in less than two months.

"Thanks, Jesus," I murmured aloud, "without You we
could never even have started." I felt a deep peace, a certainty of His nearness. There, in that muddy ditch, with His
hand on the shovel beside mine.

Why, He really is here with me, I thought. I did not have
to go to a wilderness lake or into the deep woods to seek
Jesus, wonderful as these places were. I did not even have
to retreat to my interior garden to meet Him in prayer,
helpful as that was too at times. I'd had little opportunity
for either while we were building the house, and yet He had
been beside me all summer long. I didn't have to escape
from my everyday world to be with Jesus. All I had to do
was speak His name, from whatever ditch I was standing
in at the moment, to feel His presence guiding me, guarding
me, making me whole.